LOVE NOTES TO GOD

*An American Woman's Profound Impact
on Worship in the French-Speaking World*

LINDA PANCI

G000058502

YWAM Publishing
Seattle, Washington

YWAM Publishing is the publishing ministry of Youth With A Mission (YWAM), an international missionary organization of Christians from many denominations dedicated to presenting Jesus Christ to this generation. To this end, YWAM has focused its efforts in three main areas: (1) training and equipping believers for their part in fulfilling the Great Commission (Matthew 28:19), (2) personal evangelism, and (3) mercy ministry (medical and relief work).

For a free catalog of books and materials, call (425) 771-1153 or (800) 922-2143. Visit us online at www.ywampublishing.com.

Love Notes to God
Copyright © 2015 by Linda McGowen Panci

Published by YWAM Publishing
a ministry of Youth With A Mission
PO Box 55787, Seattle, WA 98155-0787

Originally published in French as *Notes d'amour pour Dieu* (JEM Editions, 2013) and available at www.jem-editions.ch.

Unless otherwise noted, Scripture quotations in this book are taken from the New American Standard Bible®, Copyright © 1960, 1962, 1963, 1968, 1971, 1972, 1973, 1975, 1977, 1995 by The Lockman Foundation. Used by permission.

Scripture quotations marked NLT are taken from the Holy Bible. New Living Translation copyright© 1996, 2004, 2007, 2013 by Tyndale House Foundation. Used by permission of Tyndale House Publishers Inc., Carol Stream, Illinois 60188. All rights reserved.

ISBN 978-1-57658-895-6

Printed in the United States of America

To my very dear friend
Cynthia Bloomer
who went to be with the Lord during the
writing of this book.
This woman of faith, dedicated to hospitality,
was a burst of sunshine
and a constant encouragement to me.
Cynthia always saw the best in others.

Contents

Foreword

THE history of advances in missions can be read as a series of moments when a man or a woman of God saw a group of people who were not being ministered to with the gospel. It's not that other believers didn't see them with their physical eyes, but they hadn't perceived them as being important in the plan of God. So they were left out of the church's plans and projects.

Jesus "saw" children and women and foreigners. Paul saw the Gentiles, the Moravians saw unreached populations in several areas of the world. William Carey saw the language groups of India without a translation of the Bible into their tongues. The Booths saw the poor of East London. Hudson Taylor saw the populations of the teeming cities of the interior of China. Ruben Saillens saw the need to compose and translate new hymns for the French-speaking evangelical Protestants. Mother Teresa saw the dying on the streets of Calcutta, and David Wilkerson saw the gangs of New York City . . . we could go on and on.

And Linda saw the brilliant and gifted but spiritually needy people of the francophone world. Of course, she wasn't the first. Many francophones were committed to evangelism, especially from the time of the Geneva revival in the early nineteenth century and continuing on through the twentieth. In Youth With A Mission (YWAM), the Portales had preceded Linda, Greater Europe Mission had started works in the sixties already, Teen Challenge had come to Paris, and so on. Overall, Europe had again become a mission field. This was not clear to the church until the end of the twentieth century; for example, the scintillating sophistication of francophone culture masked their deep needs.

Linda started out her missionary career by doing evangelism in France. But she was quickly led to use her gifts in music and songwriting more and more. The impact of this ministry in the francophone world cannot be overstated; she and her teams helped rewrite the history of francophone missions in the late twentieth century.

A final point about Linda: this young single girl from the American Midwest who took on one of the spiritual Goliaths of this world—she had the faith to do so. As you will read in the story about the second printing of the songbook, *J'aime l'Eternel*, she was the one who had that faith. I approved her request to double the print run with no hesitation, because I knew that she had God's anointing of faith on her for this project.

Where did her faith come from? From the same source as for us all: through obedience. When we obey, our faith grows. As a matter of fact, I am convinced that each step of obedience raises our faith level a little more; and years of ongoing obedience produce men and women of God who will stop at nothing to advance His kingdom.

Linda paid the price for her ministry; and there is always a price to pay. With great openness and humility, she tells some of those stories in this book. My wife and I helped her walk through a few of them. If anything, Linda has understated the price she paid.

The principal quality that the Lord looks for in choosing His ministers is also the rarest: availability. It sounds so simple; but forty years in missions have convinced me that very few people are truly available to pay any price to do all that the Lord wants in and through them.

It is a privilege to know Linda, and now her husband Tom. They are close colleagues, respected fellow ministers, and dear friends. I commend this testimony to you; the reading of it will be worth every minute.

Dr. Tom Bloomer
International Provost of the University of the Nations
Youth With A Mission

Thank You . . .

TO MY beloved husband, Tom, for your encouragement and perseverance. Thank you for standing beside me, assuring me, and helping me to find just the right words to express my experiences.

To Eliane Lack, Jocelyne Muller, Cynthia Bloomer, and my husband Tom, the dedicated writers' group who spent hours reading and recentering the content on the essentials.

To Anne Emmett for your faithful, detailed French translation and your friendship.

To Catherine Froehlich and Betty Caloin; your work of reviewing the French text was masterful and tireless.

To Edwin Allan; you were a treasure to me as you advised me on the choice and preparation of photos and designed the original cover.

To Dominique Pelou, Micheline Le Briquer and Paul Schilliger for allowing me to print your photos in this book.

To Marvelyn Adams, who so carefully did the layout for the texts and photos.

To each one who assisted me by reading and commenting on the texts: Mary Anne Phemister, Joe Portale, Shelby Hofer, Aletha Kuenstler, Linda Johnson, Ariane de Chambrier, Patricia Cook, Tom Bloomer, Rolf Schneider, Darlene Cunningham, and my colleagues at YWAM French Publications.

To so many friends who reminded me of stories and details from our early years with YWAM and who prayed for the accomplishment of this book.

One last note is to honor my dear parents, Bob and Mable McGowen. Mom went to be with the Lord in 2008 and Dad in 2013. They were my most faithful supporters and saved over thirty years of my letters, enabling me to write with clarity about the past.

The Call

"I WANT you to go to France and write Christian songs." The words rang in my head and shook my entire being. *Could God be speaking this to my heart?*

A visiting missionary family working in French-speaking Africa had come to share at my Bible College chapel service that morning. As the father spoke of their involvements, I felt excitement building in my heart. But coming to the end of his story, he explained: "Now we must close the doors to our work because our organization thinks we are not seeing enough results." When I heard this comment, a dagger pierced my soul. Surely God was trying to get my attention.

I promised Him that as soon as I finished classes and work that day, I would find a place to pray and ask Him what He wanted to say to me through this.

After work that afternoon at the music store downtown, I went to eat supper at the college cafeteria. As I started to pick up my silverware, God reminded me of my promise. Even though I complained that my stomach was grumbling and the dining room would soon be closed, I sensed that God was tugging at my heart to listen to Him. Now.

I put my tray and silverware back. Grabbing my jacket to cut the light spring breeze, I made my way across campus to another building where a transformed bedroom had been set apart for prayer. I had no sooner knelt at a chair when God spoke these words to my heart: "I want you to go to France and write Christian songs."

There was no audible voice, but the impression was so strong that it took my breath away. I sat there stunned. *Does God really think I am capable of doing this?*

After a few minutes I tried to reason with God. He had seen how difficult it was for me to communicate in French when I was there two years ago with my uncle.

Yes, I had a French uncle! Aunt Doris, my mother's sister, had met Uncle John when she served as a missionary in Africa. The more I got to know him, the more he and his country had won a special place in my heart. The summer I turned seventeen, they invited me to go with them to visit France. We traveled from Paris to Brittany, to the Mediterranean and finally through the Alps. I discovered lively French markets, crowded French beaches, creamy French cheese, noisy, endless discussions around the table and wild French driving. I was fascinated by the diversity of this land and the uniqueness of the people, but when I tried to understand their language I felt lost and helpless. I had studied French for three years in high school, so I could say certain phrases, but they spoke so fast that I could not grasp the meaning of their words.

I continued to argue with God. "Me . . . compose in French?" When I wrote my first song in English, it had taken me hours to complete. How could I possibly do that in French?

This was my second year at Open Bible College, a small school in Des Moines, Iowa not far from my family home in Metz. I had loved music ever since I was a child. I would sit on the sidewalk outside our house and listen to my neighbor practicing her accordion almost every night. At age six my parents rented me a small accordion and I began lessons, which I continued through high school. I also picked up piano and organ, and played string bass in the school orchestra.

Now at college, I had taken every music class offered within my first two years. My composition class had begun a few months earlier and I found it hard work to write music. It was not a simple matter of inspiration. Composing was much more involved than I had imagined. Not only did I need to create a melody, rhythm and harmony, but then it had to be transcribed. It required time and effort. I naïvely thought that composers accomplished this quite easily, without much sweat. Boy was I wrong!

Back on my knees, I continued to listen, hoping God would respond to my doubts.

Silence. God said no more.

I struggled with all the implications of this being His desire for my life. *There is no way I can make this happen. I'm not fluent in French. I don't know any Christians in France. The family who spoke this morning had left their French-speaking mission field . . . and my songwriting skills are only elementary. How can I consider myself a songwriter?*

I sat back on the floor, quietly waiting for God to agree with me that I was not the person for such a task.

Realizing that God was not going to change His mind, I finally said, "OK, Lord, if you want to do this through me, I will obey and follow you. Help me believe."

A spark of excitement flittered in my heart, even though I had no idea how this could happen.

TWO

Singing God's Word

SEVERAL months later in another morning chapel service at Open Bible College, Loren and Darlene Cunningham, founders of Youth With A Mission (YWAM),[1] were guest speakers. They shared their dream about opening a fourteen-month School of Evangelism in Lausanne, Switzerland. My ears perked up. I knew this was a French-speaking area! Since that memorable day when God spoke to my heart about going to France, I had received a number of confirmations. For example, while taking a walk in the neighborhood near my college, I came across a yard sale. Among the items, there were two beautiful, enhanced watercolor prints of Notre Dame Cathedral in Paris, both at the bargain price of only fifty cents. I sensed God's spirit nudging me and bought them as a reminder of His call.

My heart leapt as the Cunninghams explained their vision: intense language study in the chosen country for the fall months, classroom

1. YWAM is a youth-centered missions organization founded in 1960 by Loren Cunningham to mobilize young people for evangelism. The first School of Evangelism was held in Switzerland in 1969.

studies on the character and ways of God during the winter months, a field trip to Israel and the Middle East in springtime, and outreaches throughout Western Europe during both summers . . . France included. Might this be the door that God was opening for me?

I took the opportunity to pray with Loren and Darlene afterwards and we really clicked. They were excited about what God had spoken to me and I was drawn by their enthusiasm and faith.

Explaining my desire to join YWAM in Europe to my Mom and Dad, however, was not quite so easy. Although I have two brothers, I am their only daughter, and in the '70s it was very unusual to let your daughter travel alone to another continent. I still remember the evening I dropped the bombshell. Daddy sat very quietly, but every part of his body language said "no way." Mother graciously asked me a few pertinent questions, easing my Dad into a more positive reflection about this new step. They finally agreed that it would be a logical program for me to follow in view of my strong interest for a ministry in the French-speaking world.

Two weeks after I graduated with a degree in Bible from Open Bible College, I walked into YWAM's training center at Chalet-à-Gobet, near Lausanne. It was a stately, old, three-story hotel on the edge of a large national forest. The view from the dining room windows was breathtaking. The majestic French Alps were standing like a backdrop behind tawny-brown Swiss cows, grazing contentedly in the field across the road, with large bells clanging around their necks.

That first day I saw Darlene Cunningham in the hallway and she exclaimed: "You finally made it! You're the gal with the long red hair from Iowa. I've been praying for you ever since we met." It had been two and a half years since I first met the Cunninghams at Open Bible College. I couldn't believe she still remembered me. What a reassuring welcome.

I began to discover the beauty of Switzerland, my new YWAM family, and the French language. Even though I had studied the language in high school, it was so helpful to live in a French-speaking country. As I left Chalet-à-Gobet with eleven other young YWAMers to study in Neuchâtel for three months, reality hit. Learning French would be a long-term process. But being immersed in the day to day experience of this culture, living and eating with a Swiss family, and attending daily French courses was the perfect way for me to learn.

Coming from the rural mid-west in the United States, I had never studied cultural differences. I had experienced living "in town" and living "in the countryside," so I was familiar with both of these lifestyles. The "Swiss way," however, added whole new dimensions. The first few months became a discovery period: learning how to ride a tram, tasting Swiss cheese (with and without holes), being greeted by young men and women with a kiss on each cheek, visiting churches of varying European denomations, and learning to value what is old over what is new.

I felt like a small child again, unable to express myself adequately, needing to be corrected and making plenty of cultural and linguistic mistakes. My most common, embarrassing mistake was to address an older person with the informal pronoun *tu* (you) when I should have been using the formal pronoun *vous*. I often felt disoriented, but was comforted by the fact that my other American friends shared the same confusing feelings of adjustment to this new country.

One Sunday after church I was invited to dinner by two Christian women and their elderly father. They were professional translators and the subject eventually came up about translating songs from English to French. They assured me that this was a complicated process, hinting that I shouldn't try it. Too late! I had already begun. In English we often sang "He is Lord," the Scripture from Philippians 2:10–11. I had looked it up in French and tried to sing it. They graciously listened to my melody and lyrics.

"*Jésus Christ est Seigneur*," I started.

"That works," they responded.

"*Il est sorti du tombeau, il est Seigneur.*"

"Yes, that's possible." Another positive reply.

"*Que tout genou fléchisse et toute langue confesse . . .*"

"Oops, far too many syllables for this phrase." They went on to suggest: "*Tout genou fléchira, toute langue confessera . . .*"

Then I added: "*que Jésus est Seigneur.*"

"*Oui* . . . yes, it works!" we exclaimed together.

"Jésus-Christ est Seigneur" became one of the first Scripture choruses that we sang at YWAM. I'm thankful for friends like these whom

God put on my path. Others followed, like Christian Glardon, an evangelical pastor and musician, who later helped us translate many lyrics into French.

After three months of language study, we returned to Chalet-à-Gobet for the lecture phase in our School of Evangelism. It was here that I learned even more about singing Bible verses. Being from many different countries and spiritual backgrounds, and without hymnals, we would simply open our Bibles and sing the Psalms.

Marion Warrington, a New Zealander, brought to us the richness of a new movement called "Scripture in Song," that was sweeping through her country. Many Scriptures were being set to music. Everyone was getting into the act, not just experienced songwriters. What a marvelous way to memorize the Bible and to keep favorite passages alive in our hearts. It was like discovering a gold mine. Singing Scripture was to become a foundation stone in our worship.

That following summer I was on an outreach team to France with about fifteen other young people. Joe and Judi Portale, the leaders of YWAM's French ministries, had contacted a local pastor who invited us to work with him, far from Switzerland in the coastal town of Kérity-Penmarch. This region is called Finistère, which means the ends of the earth. It truly is "the ends of the earth," the western-most point of the continent of Europe.

We gathered daily to pray for the village, the region and the country of France, as well as to distribute literature and make contacts with *les Bretons* (people of Brittany). I was inspired by the lighthouse, the rocks, the ocean . . . My prayer became: "Lord, make me a lighthouse, which shines brightly for You." God reminded me of Acts 13:47, which I had kept in my heart since my first visit to France six years earlier with my aunt and uncle: "I made you a light to the Gentiles, to bring salvation to the farthest corners of the earth."

I often found myself drawn to the oceanside. Some days, rather than eating supper, I escaped to the rocks only a few minutes' walk away with my guitar and my Bible. Singing Scripture to God was such a life-giving process; it drew me closer to Him. Now, for the first time, I was writing my own melodies to Scriptures in French! *God, you really can create music through me.* A sense of destiny captured my heart.

Wondering if my songs would be good enough, I made an agreement with the Lord. "If I can remember this song tomorrow, that will be my confirmation that I should share it with others." And I did! Almost every time I wrote a new Scripture song, I could still remember it the following day. I shared a few of them with Daniel Schaerer, a teacher from France who was on our team. He helped me to adjust the music to respect the rhythm and accents of the language. We actually sang a few of these songs on the streets with our team that summer.

The practice of writing melodies to Scripture was taking root among us. A year later in 1973, Joe Portale pioneered the first School of Evangelism in French. During that school at Chalet-à-Gobet and others which followed, many of our native French-speakers started putting Bible verses to music. We learned a new song most every morning!

I soon discovered other people had walked this path before me, like Pierre VanWoerden,[2] who had been composing songs to Scripture for years. Swiss hymnody was enriched by his songs for both children and adults. But he was not the first by far! I could talk about Claude Goudimel, Théodore de Bèze and Martin Luther along with other Reformers who set the Psalms to music in the sixteenth century, making Scripture more relevant to their day. If we follow this practice further back, we can trace it to those who faithfully served in the monastic tradition, singing the Psalms daily from the first few centuries through today. In the early church we find certain Scriptures from the New Testament that were sung even before they were recorded in the Bible.[3] And finally, many of the Psalms in the days of King David were sung and not merely spoken. Singing the Word of God became the first of many stepping stones on our pathway to worship. *Lord, I love to sing your Word!*

2. Pierre was a Dutch musician, the nephew of Corrie ten Boom. He and his wife came to live in Geneva, Switzerland, in 1955 and raised their family there. They served local churches, wrote numerous songs, and hosted a Christian radio program for children.

3. "Scholars make a case that the *Magnificat* (Luke 2:14), the *Benedictus* (Luke 1:68–79), the *Gloria in Excelsis* (Luke 2:14), and the *Nunc Dimittis* (Luke 2:29–32) were all hymns of the church, known and used by the church before their incorporation in the gospel text. The same has been said for the Christ-hymns such as John 1:1–18, Philippians 2:6–11 and Colossians 1:15–20 and the many psalms and doxologies such as those found in Revelation (4:8, 11; 7:12; 11:17–18; 15:3–4)." Robert Webber, *Worship Old and New* (Grand Rapids: Zondervan, 1982), 36.

THREE

To Know God Is to Trust Him

WHERE did my quest to know God begin? I first met God in a cornfield. I remember it vividly; I was fourteen years old, living with my parents and two brothers on a small farm in Iowa. I had just returned home on Sunday after an overnight stay with a friend who had taken me to church with her that morning. Bonnie told me how Jesus had become her friend. I had never heard anyone speak so personally about God and it left me perplexed. So when I got home, I went out for a walk in the field. I asked God: "What does my friend have that I don't?" The answer came through a Scripture verse that I had memorized in a summer Bible camp: "If you confess with your mouth Jesus as Lord, and believe in your heart that God raised Him from the dead, you will be saved" (Romans 10:9).

My family were not church-goers, but I had gone with different friends occasionally to the little country church on the hill just a five minute walk from my home. This Bible verse that I had learned now revealed to me how to get started in a relationship with God. So I knelt on the edge of that cornfield and prayed: "Jesus, I believe you are Lord and I believe that God raised You from the dead. Please come and live in my heart!" I was overwhelmed with joy and aware that I was being filled with new life. It was not just a dribble, but like a flow of rushing water. I was gaining a whole dimension I had never experienced before, a new perspective on life. I had been awakened to God and my friendship with Him began.

As I continued to grow closer to God during my teenage years, I read the Bible a lot. This was my best source of knowledge about Him. I am also very thankful for a couple of wonderful Sunday School teachers from my country church who explained the Scriptures to me and my friends. This group loved to get together and sing. So nine of us, including my little brother, Bob, started a music group, *The New Life Singers.* We were invited to different congregations to share our personal testimonies and songs. It was an important time of growth, and of learning to serve God as we expressed our love for Him in this way. My parents were also touched by our testimonies. The following year my Mom and Dad, both my brothers, Gerry and Bob, and I were all baptized and became regular churchgoers.

After high school I went to Open Bible College and many of the classes and people there motivated me to go still further in my spiritual walk. One of my favorite classes was "systematic theology," studying themes like salvation, Christology (the study of Christ), ecclesiology (the study of the church), and eschatology (the study of the end times). At first, I didn't even know what half these words meant! But I loved learning about God.

The teaching that marked my life most, though, was the study of the nature and character of God during my YWAM School of Evangelism (SOE) in Switzerland during 1971–72. There were around ninety of us packed into the ground floor classroom where we learned to know and experience God more deeply. YWAM's motto is: "To know God and to make Him known." This introduced a passion into my heart that would help me define my purpose in life.

I began to realize that He is a God I can understand because He made me in His image. I have the ability to think, to reason, to imagine and to remember because He made me to be like Himself. The difference is that His capacities and His knowledge are infinite; while mine are limited. There will always be more to discover about Him.

Before this, I had never grasped that God has deep emotions. He feels joy, suffers grief and disappointment and enjoys fellowship. My capacity to feel love, sadness, anger and jealousy all stem from His likeness that He put in me. He wants us all to experience life with our whole being!

My image of God expanded even more as Joy Dawson, one of our YWAM teachers, spoke to us about "The Greatness of God." I had only to step outside at Chalet-à-Gobet and meditate on the majestic mountains to be inspired by God's magnitude . . . or follow the path into the nearby forest and gaze at a wild flower to appreciate His tenderness. Joy explained: "The glory of God is the sum total of His attributes: His love, His holiness, His power, His knowledge, etc."

I reflected on the impact of these infinite qualities. I started to see how these characteristics influence each other: God's wisdom shapes His use of power, His goodness balances out His justice; His knowledge guides His expression of love. How could anything in all of life be more important than knowing God and following His ways? I love the Westminster Catechism, which states: "Man's chief end is to glorify God and to enjoy Him forever." Knowing God's character was becoming the foundation stone for our worship and would bring stability in hard times.

During this training phase I kept running into two other students in our tiny prayer room. Gloria, Dena and I always seemed to show up there at the same time. We would pray over the day's teaching and its implication in our lives, as well as share our deepest thoughts and hopes with each other. This practical way of knowing God through spiritual fellowship remains among my most precious memories.

In the last week of our SOE lecture phase, Duncan Campbell, a Scottish revivalist, came to share his story of revivals in the Hebrides Islands. While he was with us he had a heart attack, was taken to the hospital and died a few days later. I remember the wind blowing fiercely the night he passed away. Gloria, Dena and I had stayed up late into the night with others, praying for him and for the ongoing impact of his life. Who among us would continue to walk in his footsteps as men and women of God?

Don Stephens, one of our school leaders, had spoken to us a few days earlier about *counting the cost* and committing our whole lives to serve God. During the 1970s, this was a real emphasis in Christian circles. I felt in my heart that I should not stop after my fourteen month SOE with YWAM, but should continue in missionary work. I said "yes" to God's prompting.

Don's exhortation came at a very good time. Only a few months earlier I had begun to question my call to France. I had met a handsome young leader in YWAM who was headed to the Middle East. David (not his real name) and I were attracted to each other and desired to develop our relationship. But my calling had always been to France! In the last four months alone I had been there four times on evangelistic outreaches.

In seeking the Lord about this relationship, Psalm 62:5 stood out to me: "My soul, wait in silence for God *only*, for my hope is from Him." I had even prayed a tough prayer after hearing Joy Dawson's teaching on marriage: "God, do you want me to marry?" I felt He had said "Yes, but not now." However, my heart was already attached to David and I was finding it very difficult to let go. I reasoned that perhaps this was a test from God, and later He would bring our lives together. It was not easy for me to have to wait concerning this relationship, or to possibly hear a "no," but I was learning to lean on God and His reliable character.

Several months later while with a team in France, God again reminded me of my life's calling. It was August 1972, and I was still struggling with a lack of harmony in my heart. Yet God was using us to witness to many people in the city of Quimper in Brittany. Amazingly, the city council had given us a street-front meeting room to use as a coffee bar, but it needed a lot of scrubbing and paint. We called it: "Le Phare" (the Lighthouse). A number of people had turned to God and His presence was becoming more evident in this city. Towards the end of our six-week summer outreach, however, as our team was preparing to leave, I awoke one morning in a panic. What if God asked me to do something difficult, like staying in this city after everyone else on the YWAM team left? What about my family? What about my boyfriend?

My younger brother was getting married in a few weeks and I already had plans to return to the United States for the wedding. And I had just found out that my Mom was in the hospital with kidney stones. I wanted to think that my call to France was coming to an end so that I could move on to still another country and work with my boyfriend. I found myself reading the book of Job and identifying with his struggles of losing all those he loved.

Our last Sunday morning together, we gathered to worship at "Le Phare" with our team and a number of believers from the city of Quimper. In all three messages (yes, three!) a clear call was given: "the harvest is plentiful, but the workers are few." Our leader, Joe Portale, continued: "Some of us feel like Job, with all our trials. But we should be reading Jonah and stop running from our Nineveh." That was me! My response burst out: "I will not run, but I will commit myself to come back to this place if You want."

Yes, I did go to my brother's wedding. I was only in the United States for three weeks though, and thankfully able to be with my mother who was just home from the hospital recuperating from her operation. God, in His wisdom and His goodness, had allowed me to be with my family at an important time. He loves my family too!

God, in His patience, had let me see the good things He was doing in the city of Quimper even though I was still struggling over the diffi-cult choice to serve Him in France or follow my boyfriend. He remained focused on His plan for me, even when I was wavering! His faithful-ness to me was worth my trust in Him. As it was, before the summer was over, David had informed me that our relationship was over. I was heartbroken, but finally I was free to follow God.

So it was with a wounded heart that I returned to follow-up our work in Quimper. Joe Portale had asked me to be the team leader. It was mid-September; the tourists had gone, the gray season was already beginning. Our small YWAM team of five women moved into a single, unheated room above the coffee bar. We slept on mattresses on the floor and used the public baths once a week. We lacked men to help with the coffee bar and there was growing contention among us. We struggled to see if our presence was making a difference in this city.

Thankfully, God had given me a specific thought that we should *sow the seed of His Word everywhere*. So we distributed a considerable amount of literature, met young people at schools and on the streets and invited them to our coffee bar. The local pastor we were working with moved his young family from a coastal town to Quimper to be more available for the ministry. The coffee bar became a place of worship on Sunday mornings. Yes, a new church was born! The film projectionist from the cinema across the street became a believer in Christ. Objectively speaking, we were seeing God at work and He was adding to our numbers.

However those were dark months for me. I was struggling with depression and uncertainty as a leader. I was not sure that I was hearing from God and spent a lot of time crying and praying. I felt the weight of spiritual oppression as never before. Culture shock was not a concept that was taught in the early years of YWAM, but I'm convinced now that that was part of my problem . . . along with the heartbreak. A few of my team members were supportive and helpful, but others were critical and this added to my self-doubt.

Disunity unfortunately crept in, not only among my team members, but also between the pastor and other believers. There was ongoing contention and spiritual oppression. Two of my team members announced one day that they were leaving the following morning, which they did. Another team member kept making decisions that involved us all, but without consulting me. I felt like I had failed as a leader. I was very thankful when Joe Portale suggested during a phone conversation that we all plan to return to Lausanne at Christmas and let the local Christians continue this ministry.

Although some strong foundations had been laid in my heart earlier that year about the character of God, I was feeling apprehensive about returning to Lausanne. What kind of debriefing was awaiting me? Would I be looked down on because my team had fallen apart? Would God's kindness and goodness carry me through this dark phase?

FOUR

Thinking God's Thoughts

RETURNING to the YWAM center at Chalet-à-Gobet, I was relieved to be met with loving acceptance. I had expected to be "repenting" for weeks due to my perceived failures. The debriefing never happened as a team. Instead, I was able to spend time with Darlene Cunningham, who embraced me, expressing love and encouraging me to go on with God's plan for my life.

This brought a degree of healing after living out rejection by several of my team members, my boyfriend, David, who had moved on to his next mission, and worse still, self-rejection. Darlene taught me to pray: "Lord, I don't understand, but I love You and I trust You."

One evening, I remember lighting a candle in my room while praying and singing to God. I could actually feel His presence again, after experiencing numbness for months. I spent some time sharing with one of our YWAM speakers while showing her around Lausanne. This wonderful woman of God, Jean Darnall, said to me, "Your numbness to feelings has been the protection of God." *That makes sense,* I thought,

God's presence has not left me, but He has been sheltering my fragile emotions. What a kind God.

I was asked to lead the music for the current School of Evangelism and to help Joe Portale with the French mailings. I gladly accepted. As a staff member, I could attend evening lectures and I ate up the rich teaching. The Biblical principles were sinking even deeper into my heart than the year before. Psalm 32:8 says: "I will guide you along the best pathway for your life. I will advise you and watch over you." I really sensed that the Lord was my Shepherd and I could follow His leadership and plans for me. I could now lie down in these green pastures at Chalet-à-Gobet and rest. I desperately needed a safe place where my strength and my soul could be restored.

"It's like I'm starting a new life," I wrote in my diary in January 1973. I was so hungry to please God, yet I was still working my way out of depression. Unbelief was one of the big issues for me to overcome. God led me to confess this sin to my team members from the previous months. This act cleansed me from the power of negative thinking. God was purifying and renewing my heart. He was teaching me to walk in faith. Today, I understand that many of my struggles had also stemmed from disappointments, discouragement and culture shock.

Around Easter I heard Loren Cunningham speak for about the third time on the topic of "Thinking God's Thoughts." The basic message was: *The power of God is the power of creation. Why does He fill us with His Holy Spirit? So that we can think His thoughts, feel His emotions, and pray according to His desires. We can actually speak into existence the desires of God's heart. In Genesis, God created by proclaiming things that did not yet exist (i.e., "Let there be light"). We have our part in creating with God!* A foundation was being laid in my heart to have faith to create with God. This was so uplifting after the tough times I had been through.

An example of acting on God's thoughts came through my colleague, Joe Portale, who believed God was speaking to him about having a major YWAM outreach in Paris that summer. Here was the opportunity for a small group of us to participate in Joe's vision and to create something with God. Because we had no infrastructure to build on and very few team members, we visited youth groups and churches, recruiting others to join us in July. Our travels took us to Strasbourg, Forbach, Mulhouse, Lyon, Paris, Geneva, Lausanne, Yverdon, Clarens, Liège, Charleroi, and Brussels. We got more and more excited as others responded to this opportunity. Joe met several Christian businessmen from Paris who assisted us in finding a campground, tents and finances for literature.

I began to understand the importance of speaking out what God was putting in my own heart too. In May, I wrote in my diary: "I believe . . . I believe God . . . I believe God wants me to be involved in the Paris outreach and I believe He wants me to publish and record French music." *Wow, where would this lead me?*

I started walking more by faith. I was convinced that God wanted us to make a cassette of the music and some messages from the Paris outreach. I was confident that we would have the singers and the possibility of recording during this upcoming event. My biggest challenge was that I had no regular, personal financial support. Plus I would need to raise finances for cassettes and cassette duplication. Occasionally, my parents sent me a modest check and my mother made and sent me lovely clothes. These sustained my basic needs. But when I started to travel and talk about outreach, my financial needs jumped to a higher level and my faith was being duly tried. Then one day God encouraged me while we were recruiting in Belgium. A friend from a previous outreach walked up and gave me 500 Belgian francs (about $35). I was so touched. But still another test came at the end of June when Loren Cunningham told me that YWAM's tape duplicator had been sold! I wondered how we would make copies of the cassettes we wanted to record in Paris.

The Paris Outreach, July 1973, was everything and more than we had dreamed it would be as we prayed and followed God's leading each day. Three hundred and thirty young people gathered to proclaim Christ through song and testimony. Around 250,000 French Gospels of John had been printed for the event and were distributed in newspaper format in five key locations of the city. The areas our teams worked in were: Montmartre and the Sacré-Coeur Church, the Eiffel Tower, the Latin Quarter, the Luxembourg Gardens and the Champs-Elysées. Hundreds of "divine encounters" took place over those two weeks.

One afternoon in the Luxembourg Gardens, God led me to approach two sightseers from Hungary, which was still behind the "Iron Curtain." They were startled by the newspaper I had handed them and came back to ask a question: "What is happening in your world with Jesus?" I told them about the "Jesus Revolution" and the wonder of so many young people turning to God in the free world. They listened carefully. Then one of them said, "Thank you so much. I am a priest. I have been so hungry to know what our Lord is doing outside my own country."

Another story that particularly touched me was the meeting of a YWAMer with a young tourist strolling through the Tuileries Gardens. He didn't seem to be in any kind of hurry. He said he had been observing the YWAMers after he was given a Gospel. "I am not listening to you because of what is written in this paper," he said. "I am listening because of the joy written on your faces. Tell me how to get this joy." The YWAMer shared simply that he loved God and had asked God to forgive his sins. He explained that God had promised to do so because of Christ who died on the cross to pay for those very sins. He explained that he talked with God every day, learning about Him through the Bible. The young man then accepted to pray and invite Christ into his heart and ask forgiveness for his sins.

As for the music during this outreach, I had the pleasure of working with a number of friends from the School of Evangelism and other previous teams. Plus, I met several other participants who blessed us with new French and English songs. We were able to record many of them along with most of the messages. A friend put together a master tape with both music and parts of three messages to be reproduced on a ninety-minute cassette. My little home church in Metz, Iowa contributed money to help duplicate them, which we did through a ministry called Croisade (Crusade) in Geneva. I took orders from the participants for over one hundred cassettes, which were sent to them after they had returned home, all around the world. I had pledged that any profit we made would go toward the birthing of YWAM's Mercy Ships ministry. How amazing that my little church could bless the French-speaking world through their gift, and the French YWAMers could contribute to the new ship ministry by buying this souvenir cassette! I was so encouraged to see God's hand in helping us with this first production.

Also during this time, God did not overlook the issues of my heart. My ex-boyfriend showed up in Paris, leading one of the outreach teams. One morning he was asked to teach our group and his subject was relationship breakdowns and forgiveness. I was furious. I didn't feel that David had the right to speak on this subject after the way he had ended our relationship! I wrestled with God all afternoon, asking Him to remove any lingering anger. To forgive our debtors means they owe us nothing. I came to the conclusion that my only response could be to forgive him *again* for hurting me so badly.

A few days later, on a Sunday evening, we had a communion service among us. It was the perfect time for me to take the initiative to express my forgiveness to David. Thankfully he followed by asking my forgiveness for the hurt he had caused me. The circle of pain was now closed. We could both move on in our relationships. By the way, David met his wife at that outreach! I remember sharing with my girlfriend, Gloria, that I had been freed. I felt there was a large open space in my heart where God's projects could grow.

And grow they did! After the two weeks in Paris, evangelism teams were going out to different areas for another month. I believed in my heart that God wanted a traveling music team to crisscross France for the rest of the summer. I discovered that John Gordon, another YWAMer and his family, had expressed an interest to lead such a team. The last few days of the outreach the details came together for that to happen. Stella, Gloria, Ernest, Francis, and I joined the Gordons. We formed a music team that visited, performed and encouraged all of our other teams ministering in France . . . Quimper, Biarritz, Nice, Gagnières, a camp in Belgium, and "The Ark," a YWAM coffee bar on a barge, docked in one of Amsterdam's canals in Holland.

Daring to think God's thoughts and walk in faith to make things happen was becoming a lifestyle. Living with like-minded people and leaders around me prepared fertile ground to let God's seeds grow and help our dreams to become reality. What would be next?

Creating with God

"COULD I have a copy of the song you sang tonight?" I asked my friend, Régine. "The one about 'the truth, the way and the life'?" I was in southwest France with a YWAM team. We had just shared an evening of worship and testimonies with a youth group.

Régine walked over to the corner of the room and thumbed through a pile of song sheets. A few minutes later she came back, carrying a piece of paper with only words typed on it.

"Thank you, Régine, but what about the musical notes? How do you remember the melody? And how do you know what chords to play?"

"Hmmm," she said, thinking. "Let's go get the guitarist. Maybe he will know."

Thankfully he did. So I wrote down the chords over the words and did my best to transcribe the melody line without a piano. Finally, we had put together the elements of the song and I left with a cryptic musical score for the song "*Il est la vérité, le chemin et la vie*" (He is the truth, the way, and the life).

As a newcomer to Europe, I was always listening to the songs from my host countries. Although each church denomination had its own hymnal, I was searching for musical styles that would be more appealing to the youth. I found very little in print. Indeed, the common response to my request for a copy of a recent song was to receive a page with words only on it. Rarely, if ever, had someone notated the melody. Occasionally it included guitar chords. I started traveling with score paper or a tape recorder in order to transcribe and record the songs I was hearing.

In the 1970s a new move of God was sweeping across Europe with many young people showing a hunger to know Him. This "Charismatic Renewal" needed fresh expressions of worship to go along with God's stirrings. I was already aware that new songs bring new life and experiences with the Lord. What a joy it was to accompany spiritual growth through the gift of song! The treasures came not only from what my YWAM friends and I composed, but through the flood of worship that God was pouring out across the body of Christ internationally.

I had met several French songwriters who were offering new compositions to their churches, but they were not known from one group to the next. There was very little networking happening among the churches. My desire was to see their songs used by other French-speaking believers.

In May 1973, I had written in my diary: "I believe You want me to publish and record French songs." This was a growing conviction and the obvious next step in following the call of God on my life. A few months later Joe Portale, our French director came to me with a question.

"Linda, what do you think about compiling a French songbook? We could use it during our French YWAM schools." YWAM was growing very quickly and we needed tools for worship and outreach.

"Wow," I exclaimed, "I would love to do that! In fact, I already have a collection of songs that I've gathered as I've traveled with teams."

Yet, I wondered, wouldn't it be considered presumptuous for a young American woman to pursue the task of gathering and editing a songbook for French-speaking worshipers? *Surely there should be someone else more capable to do this!* I wrestled with my doubts. God, however, reminded me of what He had impressed upon me after that chapel service at Bible college. Writing French songs was not just my good idea, but a door opened by God. Recently a verse of Scripture had spoken to my heart: "Remember, dear brothers and sisters, that few of you were wise in the world's eyes or powerful or wealthy when God called you. Instead, God chose things the world considers foolish" (1 Corinthians 1:26–27 NLT). If God believed I could do this, couldn't I believe it too?

On the practical side of things, at YWAM Lausanne, I had recently assisted a colleague, Marion Warrington. She was using a rented "music-writer" to prepare songs for printing YWAM's English songbook. I knew that it was possible to follow the same process in French, but it was a daunting undertaking. The music-writer was simply a typewriter with the keys transformed from letters to musical notes and symbols, allowing a person to type the music on score paper, note by note. Afterwards, we put the musical score in a conventional typewriter and added the words underneath the notes. Finally, the third step was to paste the chords in place. If only computers had existed at that time!

I decided to go for it. It was a walk of faith as I tried to imagine what was in God's heart for this project. Publishing new songs would provide stepping stones for many to walk on as we learned to love God in worship.

Creating the French songbook was a bit like being pregnant. Initially, I had conceived the original spark of life during a time of prayer that spring, but it didn't develop into a concrete plan until my leader asked me in September to take it on. I had already been composing and gathering new songs for some time. Especially touched by the singing of Bible verses, I compiled over fifty melodies put to Scripture by French-speakers during the next two months. Jolinette Maire (now Suter) assisted me in choosing some well-loved hymns and other choruses.

An opportunity opened up for me to go to Hurlach, Germany to work on the songbook. The YWAM center there had decided to buy a "music-writer." However, they didn't know when this machine would arrive, or how long it would take for my colleague, Marion, to complete the English songbook which she had begun working on while in Lausanne.

While waiting for an answer from Germany, I made plans to go to Iowa for Christmas and stay for a couple of months. I had not returned to visit my family in the United States for over a year and I was anxious to see them again, and they me. I also intended to visit other music ministries and see how they functioned. I had hoped to go to California and meet more Christian musicians, but money didn't come in and I ended up staying in Iowa. So I interviewed everyone I could find in Iowa who was serving the Lord through music, some employed by churches, others doing it as a hobby.

An interesting twist came about when I was suddenly offered several jobs. My former Bible College proposed that I become their Dean of Women. This was a very appealing invitation. I could gain my living during the school year by advising students and spend my summers in Europe working on music with YWAM. *Hmm . . . could this be God's provision?* I wondered. I had very little financial support. My parents had been faithful over the past year to send me sufficient funds for my living expenses, but at twenty-four years old I couldn't expect them to continue to support me. So this was indeed a tempting offer! The Bible College also needed some secretarial help immediately. I accepted to fill in as a temporary secretary.

However, only a few days into the job, I read in my morning devotional, *The Daily Light,* "I am with you and will keep you wherever you go and will bring you back to this land; for I will not leave you until I have done what I have promised you" (Genesis 28:15). I was sure God was speaking to me about returning to Europe and preparing YWAM's French songbook. So after a month of work I left my job, purchased a one-way airplane ticket and returned to Switzerland. Other than my parents, I still had no promise of financial support, but I knew God was with me.

Arriving back in Switzerland at the end of March 1974, I again contacted YWAM Germany. The music-writer had arrived and I was welcome to come. I gathered together my materials and within a few weeks traveled to "the castle" in Hurlach, Germany.[1] This small castle,

1. YWAM Germany's first center is a seventeenth-century castle, which was purchased early in 1972 to lodge participants for the Munich Olympic Outreach. It pioneered YWAM's international publishing ministry.

although needing some renovations, was full of charm. I was welcomed by Marion and the staff of the graphics office, and found the work environment most encouraging. Their department was presently doing the layout for the English songbook and a professional artist was creating illustrations for it. The result was unique: songs interspersed with illustrations and pictures. This gave me many ideas for our French songbook.

One morning as I awoke, I felt this *baby* growing in me. A plan for the layout of our book came to my mind. We could organize it as described in Ephesians 5:19, "speaking to one another in psalms and hymns and spiritual songs, singing and making melody with your heart to the Lord." In the first section, we could include not only melodies of the Psalms, but all the Scriptures we were singing. The second section could feature hymns, and the third, the newer choruses that we had been singing to God. In this passage from Ephesians, the apostle Paul seems to be describing early church worship rather than advocating three strict categories. The Old Testament Psalms were an oral tradition, and were sung widely throughout church history. "Hymns" were songs with texts which honored God and Christ. "Spiritual songs" was a broad term implying songs of all kinds and styles, with the qualitative adjective, spiritual. As I prayed more the plan grew in my heart, just like an infant in the womb.

I expected our work to be completed in six weeks, but this new *baby* was not ready to be born! There was so much work involved. The actual typing was relatively quick with only the melody lines, words and chords for Scripture songs. But when I started preparing the hymns with four-part harmonies and several verses, each song could take a couple of days. My other surprise came with the correction phase. If a note was not exactly on the correct line or space of the staff, it had to be carefully retyped, glued on, and proofread again. That's why multiple re-reads were necessary. It seemed like an unending process.

I remember stepping outside our workplace into the castle garden one June night after working for hours on corrections and looking up at the starry sky. "Father God, when you made these fabulous constellations and decorated the sky with each star in place, it was perfect. You didn't need to make any corrections!" How different it is in my world. I spend more hours correcting than creating. *How can I ever finish this book?* Looking up at His heavens, I could only say, "You are an outstanding Creator! Your wisdom, your perfection and the resulting beauty are so much greater than anything I know. Please put Your fingerprint on the work of my hands, so that it can bring You much glory and pleasure."

Six weeks later, while in the train returning to Lausanne for a brief stay, I was reminded of a verse from 2 Corinthians 8:11 that God had impressed on me months earlier: "But now finish doing it also; that just as there was the readiness to desire it, so there may be also the completion of it by your ability." Two YWAM friends from Lausanne, Jolinette Maire and Lillian Rosset (now Schmidt), volunteered to accompany me for fifteen days to help finish this job. Returning to Hurlach together the following week, they wound up staying for two and a half months! This Swiss nurse and medical assistant became the *mid-wives* who helped birth the French songbook.

Another factor that prolonged this *pregnancy* was that as full-time workers with YWAM, each of us had a responsibility to serve in the community. Our job was to wash dishes. At first it was breakfast cleanup, which was relatively simple, but then it became evening meal wash-up, which took considerably more time. Being part of the community also meant attending staff meetings, morning devotions and prayer times. These extra tasks and meetings felt like a burden, especially to my helpers. It had not been our plan to integrate fully into this English/German-speaking community, but we were staying longer than planned and this is how YWAM bases function. All members are expected to work together for the common good.

We also needed to cover our living expenses, but none of us had a regular income, apart from what my parents were sending me. At this point in time, we had not learned how to raise missionary support. Like certain other missionary organizations, we did not receive a salary, but trusted God to provide our daily needs. That meant that each month we prayed and asked God to supply funds for our food and lodging, plus our personal needs, such as toothpaste. Now we were adding ministry expenses to our list. I remember even praying for money to purchase stamps to send out letters! God provided in His timing.

The following spring we were still waiting for the *baby* to arrive from Germany. It was far overdue! Although we had finished preparing the songs and most of the layout before the end of the year, the actual printing had not been done. We prayed more fervently and the *baby* was born in July 1975. We christened it *J'aime l'Eternel* (*I Love the Lord*).[2] This came from Psalm 116, one of the psalms that we were currently singing. We realized that this title expressed the reason for our songbook. That's what our worship is all about . . . *loving God*!

Its first public appearance came that same month at Eurofest, a Christian youth conference in Brussels which gathered five thousand young people from all over Europe. At that exact time, Jolinette and I were already back in Hurlach preparing songs for a supplement to our book.

Little did we know how much care this *child* would need as it grew. We had chosen to use an expandable plastic spiral rather than a firm binding, to permit us to regularly add new songs. This first addition of twenty songs was called *Chantant à Dieu* (*Singing to God*). We had been learning so much about singing to God from our New Zealander friends, David and Dale Garratt that we wanted to reflect this theme. As time went on, each new supplement became an expression of what God was emphasizing among us.

A year later, our first printing of four thousand books was almost depleted. I called Tom and Cynthia Bloomer, our new French Ministries directors, who were studying in Holland.

"Tom, we are almost out of our *J'aime l'Eternel* songbooks. What should we do? Some people are saying, 'Everyone who is going to buy it has already done so.'"

"And what do you think?" asked Tom.

"Well, I've prayed about it and I think we should reprint double the amount," I said carefully. I knew that our YWAM accountant might not be happy with this expense.

"That's a good plan," Tom replied. "Since we have set aside the benefits of our sales of the songbook to reinvest in further publications, we have the finances available. God is blessing this. Let's do it."

---

2. *J'aime l'Eternel* songbooks are available from JEM Editions (YWAM French Publications), www.jem-editions.ch.

So in the summer of 1976 we printed eight thousand copies of *J'aime l'Eternel*. Two years later there was a third edition of twenty thousand copies.[3] It was just like my experience in the beginning when I would ask, "Can I have a copy of that new song?" Everybody wanted their own copy!

3. In March 2011 we printed the fifteenth edition, making a total of 196,200 copies of *J'aime l'Eternel*, Volume 1, in print. Today (2015) there are three volumes with a total of 999 songs, and they are distributed on five continents.

Intimacy with God

O N E evening in Hurlach, Germany, where I had returned to work on yet another supplement of songs to add to the *J'aime l'Eternel,* I was struck by a lecture given in their chapel service. The speaker was emphasizing the subject of intimacy with God. He asked us: "How are you used to hearing God speak to you?" In reflecting on my regular times of listening to God, it seemed that He always communicated things I needed to correct in my life. My habitual question to God at the end of a busy day was, "Is there anything You want to show me?" As I waited before Him, I expected Him to tell me where I had sinned that day. Wanting to make sure that my heart was pure before him, I would confess my sin and receive His forgiveness. Other YWAM teachers had underlined the principle of keeping our hearts clean. But tonight's speaker added another aspect: "Does God ever say something positive to you?"

How did he know I usually only heard negative comments from God? Is he reading my thoughts? He explained that God, as our Father, loves to affirm us and not just to correct us. This was a new concept for me. How could I have lived for over ten years as a Christian without grasping this truth? When the meeting ended, we were sent out individually to listen to God and hear what He was thinking about us.

Walking outside, Bible in hand, I was curious about what God might say. Finding a quiet place, my eyes fell on Isaiah 43:1–4. "Thus says the Lord, your Creator . . . He who formed you. Do not fear, for I have redeemed you; I have called you by name; you are Mine!" *What a wonderful God who first reassures me that I belong to Him and have nothing to fear!* The Scripture continued: "When you pass through the waters, I will be with you; and through the rivers, they will not overflow you. When you walk through the fire, you will not be scorched, nor will the flame burn you. For I am the Lord your God, the Holy One of Israel, your Savior. You are precious in my sight . . . you are honored and I love you." I could hardly believe these affirming words. I felt overwhelmed by His acceptance and awed by His promises. *Could He truly love me this much?* My self-confidence soared, understanding that I was precious to Him. This experience reignited my love for God.

The amazing thing was that I already knew this Scripture. I had received it as a "life verse" while on a retreat two years earlier, after a busy summer of traveling with a music team. My Canadian friend, Gloria Black (now Perrier), and I had contacted The Sisters of Mary to ask if we could come and rest for a week at their center in Darmstadt, Germany. They responded, saying that they were hosting a retreat at that time and invited us to attend free of charge. They said they would even translate the training sessions from German into English for us. We felt very special. The only problem was that neither of us had any money to travel there.

For only the second time in my life, I suggested we hitchhike. Gloria is a beautiful blond and I had long red hair. I remember us standing near the hotel at Chalet-à-Gobet with our sign for Frankfurt and my guitar in hand. It only took a few minutes before a young man in a red sports car stopped to pick us up. Although a bit hesitant, we figured that since there were two of us and one of him, we would be OK. Besides, God had opened the door for us to attend this retreat. What's more, the young man was traveling to a town close to Darmstadt! We shared our sandwiches with him and explained why we were living in Europe. He was a fast driver and within five hours we arrived and he dropped us at a tram stop where we could conveniently continue on to our destination. Whew!

"Canaan," the name of their retreat center, was indeed a small replica of God's promised land . . . a land of abundance, with prosperous gardens, a stream and several impressive buildings. We were welcomed by these Lutheran sisters, who were wearing beige habits and white head-coverings, and shown to a lovely, quiet room for the two of us. The following morning when I opened the door, breakfast was waiting for us on a tray with a scripted note, as if from the Lord, saying: "I am waiting for you." Surprised by this gentle call, I began to understand God's invitation to walk more intimately with Him.

The Sisters demonstrated a deep contentedness in life, a dedication to intercession, and gave plenty of teaching on forgiveness and reconciliation. Being at their home was like taking a drink of fresh, cool water after a long, hot summer day. The beauty and the kindness of those around me spoke deeply to my inner being and helped me to regain strength and perspective.

Near the end of our stay, we were invited to pick a card on which a verse of Scripture was written. This was to be our *life verse*. Mine was Isaiah 43:1–4, the exact same verses that I turned to that night in Hurlach two years later while seeking God's thoughts about me! This Scripture continues to accompany me through life's high waters and assures me of God's personal care. I put it to music several years later and still sing it as an exhortation for my heart not to fear, but to remain in His love.[1]

Besides listening to God through Scripture, other stepping stones to intimacy that were emphasized during our week with the Sisters of Mary was their appreciation of nature and their use of symbols. The simplicity, attractiveness and unadorned beauty of Canaan, the Sisters' home, were very intentional. They blessed their land both in prayer and by hard work. The gardens bore luscious fruit, well-formed vegetables

---

1. *J'aime l'Eternel*, no. 334. Recorded on CD, *Pour le Louer*, Volume 3. Available at www.jem-editions.ch.

and gorgeous flowers, much as I would have imagined the Garden of Eden to be. They created "the way of the Cross" on their grounds, where sculptures and landscaping illustrate the last days of Christ, with benches to sit on and meditations to read. Their use of nature and symbols corresponded so well to my personality and revived my soul.

I can't express how much God's creation has played a key role in awakening my heart to Him all throughout my life. Nature walks are an ongoing way for me to connect with Him. While living at our YWAM center in Chalet-à-Gobet, I would often escape from the busy community life to walk in the forest next door. When I teach on worship, I often invite the participants to join me outside: "Come, take a praise walk with me in the forest . . . see the height of the trees, hear the songs of the birds, breathe deeply the fresh scent in the air as it fills your lungs. Pick a tiny strawberry from the side of the road and taste its sweetness. Touch the soft new growth on the pine tree." All of nature exhibits God's handiwork, His creative mind, His abundance, and His goodness. It reaches parts of my soul that words cannot, and awakens my heart to love God.

Another helpful way to draw close to God is by setting time aside for spiritual retreats. I enjoyed assisting my friend, Eliane Lack and her late husband Rudi, to lead Easter and Advent retreats. During this time we made use of nature and symbols to grow in our communication with the Lord and with each other. Places like the YWAM center in Einigen, Switzerland, have been perfect to discover the beauty of God's creation and to nurture intimacy with Him. The Reformed sisters at Saint-Loup's diaconesses' community in Pompaples, Switzerland, have also developed an inspiring retreat center, which includes a nature walk based on the Lord's Prayer.[2]

In 2008 I audited a class at Wheaton College called "Spiritual Formation," which was an eye-opening study on different types of Christian spirituality that have been practiced throughout history. It was so refreshing to experience the spiritual exercises from the Desert Fathers, the contemplative monks and the Celtic traditions. Gary Thomas, a well-known Christian writer says, "Why should everybody be expected to love God the same way?"[3] God knows that we are not all the same, but

2. The Reformed Community of Deaconesses of Saint Loup: www.saint-loup.ch.
3. Gary Thomas, *Sacred Pathways* (Grand Rapids: Zondervan, 2000), 16.

each one of us has a unique spiritual temperament. Some people love celebrations with lots of instruments, voices and dance. Others prefer quiet meditation, or rituals, or art. Many appreciate the depth of using God's Word to come close to Him. The truth is that all these pathways can lead us to greater spiritual intimacy. God draws us to Himself and offers us freedom to relate to Him with our preferred love language.

Another thing that softens and opens my heart to commune with God is to *sing to Him*. I can't count the number of times I have sung: "Thou art my God and I will praise Thee; Thou art my God, I will exalt Thee . . ."[4] I'll always remember the day David and Dale Garratt were leading worship at Chalet-à-Gobet. I was watching them and realized that their eyes were closed as they sang. *How unusual to stand in front of people and not look at them,* I thought. David then said, "Sing directly to God. Closing your eyes or standing up might help you to focus on Him." It was surprising, because up to that time we sang songs mostly about God and always with our eyes open. I closed my eyes and started singing. It dawned on me: *I am communicating directly with God . . . and He is looking at me!* What a wonderful way to experience loving God.

These friends from New Zealand were leading us into a new dimension as personal worshipers and lovers of God. Blocking out all distraction, we focused on communing with our divine Lover. From Old Testament times, the psalmists have instructed us:

> Sing to the LORD a new song;
> Sing to the LORD, all the earth.
> Sing to the LORD, bless His name. (Psalm 96:1–2)

This truth of direct communion with God through singing had not yet influenced our YWAM worship style, but it was becoming a foundation stone of the worldwide praise movement.

Personally, it's not just singing to God while in a group at church that enhances my relationship with Him, but also singing and making melody in my heart throughout the day. As I let myself make up a melody with or without words, my thoughts are directed to God and I

4. Psalm 118:28–29 by Tony Hopkins, *J'aime l'Eternel*, no. 189 (Scripture in Song, 1972).

am aware of His presence. I was fascinated to discover this practice in 1 Corinthians 14:15: "I shall sing with the spirit and I shall sing with the mind also." Paul could be saying to us that we don't have to use words! We can simply hum a melody to Him as a way of staying in communion with His Spirit.

Earlier, I made reference to Ephesians 5:19 where Paul talks about psalms, hymns and spiritual songs. A church historian, E. Werner, reports that there was a kind of wordless hymn that was in vogue in Jerusalem during Paul's lifetime.[5] He is possibly referring to *singing in the Spirit*, which can be done spontaneously, alone or in a group.

Then we learned to lift our hands to God as an offering of ourselves (Psalms 134:2; 141:2). After that came the beautiful practice of dancing before God and using creative movement. We witnessed an explosion of expressions of all kinds in our worship. If King David could dance and use every known instrument of his day to worship God, why should we not do the same? I define worship as "giving everything that I am, to love and proclaim everything that God is." Worship includes giving something to God. As each of us contributes our talents to love and lift up the name of our God, we express the magnificence of His glory.

Early in my missionary service, I met Roxanne Brant and read her book on ministering to the Lord. She says: "Worship brings us into God's presence and brings God's presence into us . . . it is as we minister to Him that He will turn and minister to us and through us and a lifeflow will be established."[6] This is not an automatic blessing formula! It's a relational approach to living intimately in the pleasure of God's company and it can be an ongoing lifestyle. He is my reward, not only His blessings or benefits. I don't always feel His presence, nor can I continuously pursue Him, but I often make the choice to focus on His qualities and not on my frailty. Intimacy involves believing in God, receiving His love and expressing our affection and devotion to Him.

From those early days in Hurlach, Germany, I am still learning to

---

5. E. Werner, "Music," in *The Interpreter's Dictionary of the Bible*, vol. 3, ed. George Buttrick (New York: Abingdon, 1962), 466.

6. Roxanne Brant, *Ministering to the Lord* (Naples, FL: Outreach for Christ, 1973), 18.

listen to God's encouragements. One special word from Scripture that speaks deeply to my heart is Song of Songs 2:14.

> O my dove, in the clefts of the rock,
> In the secret place of the steep pathway,
> Let me see your form,
> Let me hear your voice;
> For your voice is sweet,
> And your form is lovely.

What an amazing thing that God loves to hear my voice . . . and to look at me! He actually enjoys my presence as much as I enjoy His.

*Linda with
brothers,
Gerry & Bob*

*McGowen
Family, 1960*

*Linda plays for
a talent show*

*Metz Church
in Iowa*

*Stella (Rochat)
Cau & Linda*

YWAM Lausanne Center at Chalet-à-Gobet, 1971

Loren & Darlene Cunningham, with Karen & David

Summer team in Brittany, France 1972

Joe Portale teaching

Classroom at Chalet-à-Gobet

Paul Schilliger

Maurice Ray, pastor and YWAM teacher

Duncan Campbell during SOE 1972

Eiffel Tower in Paris

Marti, Patricia & Linda singing in Paris

Campground at Paris Outreach, 1973

Small group praying in park

Jolinette, Linda & Lillian travel to Hurlach

YWAM Castle at Hurlach, Germany, 1974

Don & Deyon Stephens, YWAM leaders

La machine à musique

J'aime l'Eternel songbook

Edwin Allan

New Zealanders, David & Dale Garratt, lead worship, 1975

Worshiping on outreach

Life in Teams

COMMUNITY living! From the beginning of YWAM
we have lived together as a Christian community, most of the time in
the same building. This lifestyle has produced many blessings and just
as many headaches. Whether at Chalet-à-Gobet in the former Hotel du
Golf (our first YWAM center), in Brittany with a team of five women
in one room, or traveling with a team of twelve, the same challenge was
ever present. . . . How can we live together in peace, function well, all
while knitting our gifts and talents together to honor God and demonstrate the beauty of the body of Christ? Every team became a new
opportunity for God to build character in our lives as we collaborated
in the work of His kingdom.

In the summer of 1975, many European YWAMers gathered in
Amsterdam for an outreach. I was so pleased that among the three hundred participants, over a third were French-speakers. We were taking our
place to proclaim the Good News about Jesus! Following two weeks of
training and evangelism in the city, smaller groups were formed to serve

across Europe for the month of August. I hand-picked a small music team which would travel together and plug into other summer teams working in French-speaking countries. Sue (USA), Rosemarie (England), Walter (Switzerland), Philippe (France), and I met in Lausanne. We piled our luggage, a tent for the girls, and our musical instruments into a small five-seater Volkswagen, which would carry us to each destination.

The first day on the road we stopped to picnic in the Haute Savoie of France. We ate our sandwiches with the beauty of the Alps surrounding us and each one shared a chapter from their life, essentially how Jesus had become real to us. Listening to the stories, we understood how God had shaped our lives individually and we were looking forward to serving Him together.

Just a week earlier in Amsterdam, Floyd McClung, a YWAM leader and author, had taught us some principles about living in unity. He shared from Ephesians 4:2–3, underlining the importance of accepting, affirming, and encouraging each other by standing together in times of need. He also gave room for exhorting and speaking the truth if correction was needed.

That evening there was some tension as the guys struggled to set up the tent in the wind and menacing rain. We had already been slowed down by many vacationers on the small mountain roads and we were concerned about making our connection the following day for the ferry to Corsica, where we would meet the YWAMers working there.

One of my team members came to me saying, "Linda, I don't think this team will work."

"What do you mean?" I asked.

My colleague sighed. "We have so many kilometers to travel in this small car and no assurance it will hold up. And you see that each one of us has his own personal struggles, and . . ."

Remembering Floyd's teaching, I responded to him, "I know we could encounter problems, but God has led us together for this month. Let's walk by faith."

Afterwards, a bit shaken, I thought, *How can we possibly achieve our goals if this teammate pulls out?* He was our driver! I prayed earnestly that God would keep us all safe and confident. Reona Peterson (now Joly) had also taught us in Amsterdam: "Faith is not mental gymnastics, but rather it's knowing and trusting the character and promises of God." We needed to live this out.

The next morning we rose early and drove over the mountains south to Nice, just barely making it in time to leave our car with a local pastor and jump on the boat to Corsica. Even though we had some tense moments making this deadline, we were going ahead with faith in our hearts and gaining confidence that God's helping hand would be with us along the way.

We found the YWAM team in Corsica camping in a field. They explained that their host had surprisingly not prepared anything for their arrival a few days earlier. Daniel Schaerer, the team leader, had also chosen to go ahead by faith and trust God to use this situation to further His kingdom. We made our meals over a campfire and washed in the nearby stream, but everyone was a good sport about it. The funniest situation was the improvised toilet. Somewhere our friends had found a chair with a broken-out seat. They dug a deep hole behind some tall bamboo plants to shield themselves from public view, and set the chair over it. *Et voilà*, each one could "do his duty" without fear . . . except for the risk of falling in the hole!

One afternoon, a surprise awaited me as I picked up my air mattress and found a huge spider. "Rosemarie!" I cried. "Look at this! Is it a tarantula? Did I sleep on it all night?" Horrified, she helped me kill the creature, and we checked under her air mattress and those of the other women in our tent. We now knew to check our sleeping bags each evening before crawling in to make sure we had no other visitors.

Every morning we gathered together to worship God in song and to pray. After the heat of the day had waned, our two teams would travel to the nearby town to sing in the streets and share our testimonies. We were able to spread seeds of the gospel in several towns on this island. One big answer to prayer was that the local Catholic priest spontaneously opened up his church for Daniel's team to come and perform a play they had written. Despite the rustic conditions, their team managed to stay for the entire month of August and saw God at work in the lives of the people they met.

As initially planned, we retraced our steps after five days, picked up our car in Nice and connected with some English-speaking YWAMers who were evangelizing on the beaches there. Joining them, we took out our guitar and started singing, and vacationers gathered around us to listen. This gave us many opportunities to talk with others about Christ.

A few days later we traveled on to Marseille, joining an Egyptian YWAM team for a day. From there we went on to a Christian Camp at Gagnières in the south of France, then to Laon in the north of France, to Marche-en-Famène in Belgium, to Luxembourg and finally back to Switzerland to sing at a Christian children's camp. We had no vehicle breakdowns and lived out great team harmony in spite of the many long hours on the road. Our singing reflected our joy and good relationships. God had blessed us, honoring our faith and desire to spread His Good News. And that team member who had struggled with doubts replaced them with joy and faithful service.

In February my Swiss colleague, Heinz Suter, gathered another music team together with the purpose of recruiting young people for the upcoming 1976 Summer Olympic Outreach in Montreal. We rented La Maison de la Croix-Bleue (the Blue Cross house)[1] in the village of Servion to have a place to live and practice. This was the second winter I had lived in this tiny, snow-covered village in the Swiss countryside. The previous year I spent several months there with a small team of YWAMers who had prepared and recorded our first cassette of Scripture songs, *J'aime l'Eternel.* Although we had made some friends in the village, it always seemed isolated and snowed-in, far from the city and from a piano. I would walk to the small church where I could arrange vocal parts using the little church organ, for which I was grateful.

In this year's team, along with Heinz and myself were Hélène, Corinne, Philippe, Beth, Lidia and our technician, Guy. We would be traveling with a fabulous multi-media presentation consisting of one thousand slides ingeniously timed and intertwined, using eight projectors and an eight-meter wide screen. I had been working on arrangements of songs and praying about finding a way to take a piano accompaniment with us. Portable keyboards did not yet exist in 1976 . . . imagine! Most of our songs could be accompanied by Heinz and Philippe on guitar and saxophone, but one song needed more. If only

---

1. This was a big house belonging to the Blue Cross, an association which helps recovering alcoholics.

we could make a recording of the piano music, then we could sing along with it during the tour. Technically speaking, we would have the sound equipment necessary to play it back.

Then one day during my prayer walk, I noticed a big beautiful grand piano sitting by the front room window of one home. After praying with the team about the idea, two of us screwed up our courage and went to knock on the neighbor's door.

"Hello, I'm living with a music group for a few weeks here in Servion. I have seen your beautiful grand piano through the window and was wondering if we might be able to record a song on it." This was an extremely *un-Swiss* thing to do!

"Oh goodness, I don't know if it's in tune," the couple answered, covering the shock of such a strange request. But they graciously invited us in to try the piano and a few days later we recorded the accompaniment for "*Vous serez mes témoins*,"[2] which became our theme song.

Success! We performed in auditoriums and churches from northern France to Paris, Bordeaux, Toulouse, Lyon, in Alsace, Belgium, Luxembourg, and ten locations in Switzerland over the next six weeks. How we were able to maintain the pace of travel to these twenty-five locations, needing three to five hours each time to install the equipment and have a sound check, was nothing short of a miracle. One helpful element was that we were convinced of our mission. Also, the program was almost identical every evening and each person in the team had found his place and we were all pulling together. At the end of the tour we scheduled two days of rest and fun in the peaceful mountain village of La Côte-aux-Fées. We just didn't want to leave one another.

Four from that group then joined me in Hurlach, Germany to prepare a new addition of songs, *Enseigne-nous* (Teach us), for our French songbook. Then in early June most of them joined with the YWAM Lausanne staff to record our second cassette, *Gloire à ton nom Jésus*.[3]

The icing on the cake came in July as we welcomed 180 young missions-minded French-speakers to the Montreal Olympic Outreach. I had flown to New York just hours prior to the others. My heart

2. *Ye Shall Be My Witnesses* by Jerry Kirk (Lillenas Publishing, 1963).

3. English: *Praise the Name of Jesus*. This recording is available in French at www.jem-editions.ch.

overflowed with joy as I greeted our YWAM friends and students arriving from Europe. Many of them had heard of this opportunity through our March multimedia tour.

We waited several hours for everyone to arrive and still had to wait longer for the busses which would take us to Canada. To pass the time, several of us took out our guitars and started worshiping God, singing many of our French songs. Airport authorities didn't know what to think, but our joy and love for God spoke louder than words and they permitted us to continue. At one point a YWAM leader offered me a ride in a car, which would have allowed me a quicker trip and a good night's sleep after our transcontinental flight. But I decided to stay with our European team members, since I was welcoming them to my continent, many for the first time.

The outreach in Montreal proved to be a real physical challenge. We arrived in the small town of Dunham, Canada, 85 kilometers (53 miles) southeast of Montreal, and discovered our sleeping conditions. There were seventeen hundred participants from fifty-three nations. About two hundred of us were crowded into the large classrooms of a former school, but with no beds. We were the more fortunate ones; others stayed in tents, trailers, and in a large ice hockey arena, which was lined with the sleeping bags of seven hundred young women! YWAM was collaborating with forty-seven other Christian organizations, called Aide Olympique, in an effort to coordinate our endeavors during the Olympic Games. We would travel to Montreal every other day to pass out literature and to witness. I led a French choir which sang on the streets; others performed skits, dances, and open-air theater. We even had a Bluegrass trio from Europe that was very popular.

The spiritual battles were intense. I wrote my parents: "This is NO VACATION! We need prayer support. Please ask the church to pray every day for us." The simplest things were difficult to accomplish. For example, my colleagues and I had prepared a song sheet to be used for bilingual worship before we left Switzerland. Try as we might, the logistics were too complicated and we were unable to get it printed to use for worship during the Olympics. What a disappointment! However, we later found a printer and were able to use the song sheets as we served in multiple teams around Quebec that summer.

Another spiritual challenge that we encountered near the Olympic grounds was the Hare Krishna sect. As we worshiped and performed, they tried to disrupt us. Wearing their long, orange robes they would walk among us, trying to drown out our songs with their chants. We did not relent, but continued daily. They became angry and started physically attacking our YWAMers. One of our young women, after being struck in the face, kept turning the other cheek. Each time she told the sect member that she loved her and would not retaliate.

While we were in Montreal, Joy Dawson gave a message on "Suffering, Grace, and Glory" that deeply impacted me. We could make immediate application as we were subjected to spiritual attacks and were sleeping on hard floors. She explained that there will be situations where we will endure suffering. Our goal is not to avoid it at all cost, but to receive God's grace to go through it. As we embrace His grace during physical or emotional turmoil, we can then experience His presence and even see His glory poured out on us. The beauty of Jesus will become more evident in our lives as His Spirit lifts us above our struggles and helps us to keep our eyes fixed on Him.

The apostle Paul supports this thought: "But we all, with unveiled face, beholding as in a mirror the glory of the Lord, are being transformed into the same image from glory to glory, just as from the Lord, the Spirit" (2 Corinthians 3:18). This is not just a magic formula for getting through difficult times, but rather a walk of faith, bringing God's presence and power into our trials. Regardless of the opposition we met, our testimonies went out to this "world in miniature" at the 1976 Olympics.

In early August, after the Olympic torch was quenched, ten of us plugged into a spiritual renewal happening among the Catholics. It was exhilarating to discover God's move among these French Canadians and to bring back some of their worship songs to Europe.

Then in September I left Canada to travel with a team of friends through the United States, speaking in churches about our ministry in the French-speaking world. We even made it to my little country church in Metz, Iowa. It was the end of a very active summer and I was beginning to feel very fatigued and vulnerable. Our US team was made up of three women and two men. What I didn't realize at the time was that my four co-workers were beginning to relate to each other as couples and would soon be dating and get married! I felt left out and found myself vying for my place in the team. I finally figured out the dynamic of what was happening and later could rejoice with my friends, but at the time it was painful emotionally.

That year I worked in eight different traveling teams, mostly musical. The last one was a choir of thirty-three members, formed of students from the French-speaking School of Evangelism, the French Language School and some other YWAM staff in Lausanne. I wrote in my journal, "They are a joy to work with, even if many of them don't read music." Our choir performed as far away as Strasbourg, presented an open-house Christmas program for two hundred neighbors at Chalet-à-Gobet, and sang regularly for our Sunday evening meetings.

The year 1976 was also when YWAM expanded these worship gatherings by renting the auditorium at the Hotel School next door to us. We had totally outgrown the Chalet-à-Gobet classroom. People were coming from all over French-speaking Switzerland! Two hundred and fifty people showed up for our first night at the Hotel School and within months our numbers reached to over five hundred.[4]

Earlier that year God had given me a full-time Swiss helper, Louise. She was such a blessing to me. Together we translated, transcribed and arranged many songs, as well as creating musical events. I had now been in Switzerland for six years and was continually recruiting young people for musical projects and various teams. I never could have achieved so much without the help of many others.

The time had come to better define our music ministry. We set our goals: to glorify God, to edify the body of Christ, and to communicate the gospel message to our world through songs and artistic expressions. The bottom line was to give praise to our Creator both personally and as a group. Passages in 1 and 2 Chronicles had instructed us on how the Levitical musicians in the Old Testament functioned.[5] Building on this

4. Ten years later, we began renting the cinema of Beaulieu in downtown Lausanne every other Sunday night to accommodate the growing gathering of Christians for worship, teaching, and fellowship. These praise gatherings continued for another ten years in Lausanne with over nine hundred people in regular attendance.

5. 1 Chronicles 15:16–29; 16:4–37; 23:5, 27–32; 25:1–8; 2 Chronicles 5:12–14; 20:20–22; 29:25–31.

foundation of praise, we formed worship groups, then published and recorded new songs for the body of Christ. Through outreaches, like in Paris and Montreal, we proclaimed the gospel to unbelievers. Before long we would take on bigger projects, requiring even more faith and still greater teamwork.

EIGHT

Living Out the Prophetic

FRANCE has had a special place in my heart ever since I first visited this beautiful country with my aunt and uncle when I was sixteen. As a young Christian, I was surprised that I did not meet other evangelical believers during that six-week trip. While on a walk in the neighborhood where my uncle's family lived in a suburb of Paris, I did find a small church. But there was a note on the front door, which I understood even with my limited French: *Fermé le mois d'août pour les vacances* (Closed for vacation during the month of August). I felt shocked and disappointed. Later, I understood that some of the small churches take a break during summer vacation. This experience, however, gave me a burden to pray for the country.

Now in 1976 I found myself praying and fasting weekly, asking for God's blessing on France and the believers there. Youth With A Mission was not yet officially established in France, although we had traveled there numerous times with musical and evangelistic teams. I sensed that God wanted us to create a musical presentation based on the message of 2 Chronicles 7 to take to the churches. A couple of colleagues joined me to pray over this idea. This text became a motivating word that would spur us on for two years. After hearing a choir presentation we put together on this theme, Don Stephens, our Lausanne director at the time, encouraged us to take it further, "perhaps to France." He did not know that we had been praying specifically for that opportunity!

Returning to the village of Servion in January 1977, four of us met to study and pray through the text, 2 Chronicles 7:14, "If my people who are called by My name humble themselves and pray, and seek my face and turn from their wicked ways, then I will hear from heaven, will forgive their sin, and will heal their land." Not only did we need inspiration from God, but we as a team needed to learn to live out the message together . . . humility, prayer, personal righteousness, repentance, living as God's family and interceding for the nation. We invited God to be at work in our lives.

Knowing that no one of us had all the resources to create this performance, we asked God to give us new music and creative ways to express the message. I remember struggling to write new songs. Then I noticed God's hand on my colleague, Rolf Schneider, a young French musician who had joined us after finishing his School of Evangelism. He seemed to write a new song every day! I realized that I needed to let him do it. I could serve him by transcribing and arranging them. One day we invited Alain Burnand, a well-known Swiss pastor and songwriter, to critique our work. Rolf sang a couple of his compositions. Typical of his visual orientation, Alain pulled out the biggest coin from his pocket, threw the five Franc piece in the air and then caught it. Pointing to Rolf, he exclaimed, "The songs of this man have value and potential!" Thus we began discovering the natural gifting in each of our team members.

Then there was Louise, my faithful co-worker, who was so gifted in visual arts and music. As soon as we realized that we would need costumes, she offered to put her talent as a professional seamstress into action. She designed and sewed beautiful long dresses for each of the girls and tunics for the guys, using the colors indicated for the Old Testament tabernacle.

Another team member, Hélène, came to me one morning, frustrated because I had expressed an idea for some stage movements. But we had delegated that domain to her. I understood that I needed to back off and let her develop the choreography. She was able to visualize and demonstrate the message through scenes, dances and movements that would be adapted to the number of teammates who would join us.

In March, Marlyse joined us to assume the role of administrative coordinator. We needed such a capable and encouraging person to keep us organized. We were learning to honor and trust the gifts of God in each other, and to function as God's family.

The weeks of creation were a continual discovery process as the five of us prayed over these verses, imagining how we could communicate this message in an original way. We were challenged to think beyond our normal expressions of songs and preaching as we began to live out this prophetic word from God.

We had three major hurdles to get over, however, before we could go on tour. One was knowing how to communicate with Christian leaders in France. The second was how to organize a tour without any finances. Thankfully, YWAM Lausanne provided us with address lists and paid for three hundred letters to be sent to French pastors, explaining the vision. Then a friend loaned us a minibus so Rolf could travel to meet them and plan our anticipated tour, which was only a few months away.

But how do you explain such a presentation? We had no recording to give an idea of what the music would sound like. In fact, we were still in the process of composing it and inventing movements! Church leaders were unfamiliar with the term, "a musical," and found it difficult to grasp how a Christian group could transmit a message primarily through song and choreography. Amazingly, the pastors believed Rolf, even though most of them did not even know YWAM, trusting us to bring a word from God's heart. Rolf's walk of faith opened many doors for us. He literally left on his trip with only a tankful of gas and a few Swiss Francs in his pocket. Miraculously, God provided for his travel needs day by day.

The third challenge was that the team we would travel with did not yet fully exist! We were praying and inviting other YWAMers to join us in April. We knew that many of them would complete their SOE Field Trip at that time, but we had no assurance they would come. Plus we needed time with the enlarged group to prepare so we could leave on tour by May 1.

In mid-April another miracle happened. We were overjoyed to welcome Claire-Lise, Liliane, Ruth, Roseline, Corinne, Serge, Daniel, Walter, Marcel and David, who joined our group of five at Chalet-à-Gobet. Rolf was our team leader while Hélène and I were responsible to train them for the performance. Learning the music and movements took time, but our greatest stress factor was gathering the necessary equipment for such a tour. We were able to purchase a used electric piano, the first of its kind, from Gil Bernard, a well-known French Christian performer. It came with its specially made wooden box for travel, which took four people to carry! Some local Christians loaned us a small bus, microphones and lights. YWAM Germany loaned us a sound system. On May 1st we did our premier presentation of *Si mon peuple* (*If My People*) at Mulhouse in eastern France, where the youth of the area were already gathered for a May Day celebration. Our performance was a hit!

Twenty presentations followed. We traveled from Alsace to the north of France, stopping in seven different cities, arriving finally in Paris for five more shows. Then we journeyed on to Brittany and the south of France, back through Lyon, completing our tour in Lausanne at the end of June. While performing in Paris, four of our concerts were held in specific churches and were relatively well attended by their members. But for the fifth evening we had rented the Centre Maurice Ravel with three hundred seats, inviting all the churches to come together. Sadly, only thirteen people showed up. We were *really* disappointed. One very important goal of this musical was to bring God's people *together* to worship Him in unity.

Among those present that night was our French Ministries leader, Tom Bloomer, who had come from Switzerland to encourage us. We faithfully gave our all for those thirteen people, but in our hearts we were weary and discouraged. The following morning, Tom exhorted us not just to continue our tour as planned, but to pray about extending our commitment. He felt the impact of this message had not yet reached its full potential and that we should return to Paris in the future and expand our vision to include still other cities until this musical message had penetrated the body of Christ.

During our time in Brittany, our team took time to pray and fast about prolonging our commitment and organizing another tour. When we asked God about returning to Paris, one of our team members prayed: "Lord, don't open us a small door at the end of a street, but a large door!" Seventeen months later we did go back to Paris, renting the hall, *Wagram*, where over one thousand people came! This became a landmark moment which set the scene for YWAM ministry in France. We ended up doing two more tours, seventy presentations in all, in Belgium, Switzerland, and France.[1] A door also opened for us to perform in the protestant Cathedral of Lausanne, and it was filled!

I cannot emphasize enough the work of God in each of our lives as we toured with the message of *If My People*. The first theme of the musical was humility. This virtue presented our team with an ongoing challenge, as we had different personalities and maturity levels which were tested by the small amount of personal space that we had as we traveled and performed. When Tom Bloomer visited us in Paris, he warned us: "You are fighting in a spiritual battle. The enemy of our souls would like to use relational conflict to hinder your message. So be watchful."

This was a timely word as I had been struggling with one of our team members. I remember feeling put down by her on several occasions. In speaking with her about it, she couldn't grasp that I had felt hurt by her sharp words. Knowing that our relationship would speak louder than our words on stage, we decided to spend regular time together just to chat over tea, which improved our communication. The team made a daily effort to work out our differences and to forgive one another. This intentional fellowship built our trust in each other. Rolf also received insight to defuse numerous conflicts and to keep us centered on our goals.

Another facet of "walking the talk" was learning to live as God's people. A Bible passage that had been shaping my thoughts since early

---

1. *France*: Mulhouse, Colmar, Strasbourg, Saint-Avold, Forbach, Henin-Beaumont, Lille, Lens, Paris (7 times), Quimper, Uzès, Nîmes, Saint-Laurent-du-Pape, Lyon, Aix-en-Provence, Reims, Béthune, Narbonne, Perpignan, Montbéliard, Grenoble, Poîtiers, Bordeaux, Saint-Etienne, Meyzieu, Lons-le-Saunier, Vesoul, Marseille, Privas, Portes-les-Valence, Valence. *Switzerland*: Vevey, Lausanne, Moutier, Couvet, Geneva, Corcelles, Neuchâtel, Yverdon, Saint-Croix, Tramelan, la Chaux-de-Fonds, Nyon, Montreux, Fribourg, Berne. *Belgium*: Charleroi, Brussels, Liège.

that year says that Christ was made sin for us, that we could become the righteousness of God in Him and not live for ourselves, but for Him (2 Corinthians 5:14–15, 21). Living in His righteousness meant not only asking for forgiveness, but also receiving God's righteousness as a gift. His intention was for us to walk rightly and to give ourselves daily for others. This verse gave me the strength to believe in the power of Christ's righteousness in myself and in others.

During the months of preparation at Servion, we had received an image of us all standing in a big circle around the cross of Jesus. Here we were all equal, all needing forgiveness and all loved by the Father. As we gathered with Christians in different cities, this spiritual picture reminded us that we were on common ground with our brothers and sisters in Christ. There was no place for haughtiness or judgment. There was enough room around the cross for each one to approach the Father through Christ for forgiveness and healing.

Living out the aspect of being the people of God was one of my favorite parts of the musical. Rolf had composed a song, "*Oui, nous faisons partie de la famille de Dieu*" ("Yes, we are a part of God's family"), which we taught to audiences. Then we would take time to go out and personally greet them, encouraging them to also welcome and accept one another as God's family. How many times did the people of a city tell us, "This is the first time we have come together as believers"?

Intercession was another main theme of this musical. A wonderful man of God from New Zealand, Ken Wright, who had often taught at Chalet-à-Gobet, prayed for us before we left on tour. He challenged us to intercede for each of the cities and churches we would be visiting over the following months. This became a concrete goal that opened our spiritual eyes to the needs of each place. I am convinced that praying specifically over each city helped us to identify with the local body of Christ and gave us authority to speak out our message. What a delight it was to see the French Christians joining this movement of intercession for their towns and their nation. Together we were learning how to pray for specific domains where God wanted to plant His kingdom in a deeper way. This experience of carrying the people of God and their cities in our hearts has had an impact on my life forever.

How then do we deliver a prophetic message like 2 Chronicles 7:14

to God's people? Floyd McClung had taught us a few years earlier about becoming spokesmen for God, that is, being inspired by God to speak publicly for Him. In the Bible, prophets were usually called to speak truth to a nation. Even if a word was strong or negative, the goal was to redeem, to call people back to God. In March of 1977, while Rolf was meeting with pastors before our first tour, he sent a letter to our small team at Servion. "The Lord is showing me that we will be His prophets in the country of France and we must be sensitive and available to bring His word to His people. There are many delicate situations and divergent tendencies. We must pray fervently. Our responsibility is to deliver this message of 2 Chronicles 7:14 to the believers in France. The future of YWAM in these cities depends a lot on the outcome of this tour."

Being God's mouthpiece was not an easy road to travel. The tours themselves were strenuous and the spiritual pressure was sometimes overwhelming. Rolf remembers that in one city he was not able to finish his message because of the oppression caused by disunity among the churches there.

What then were the blessings and results that came from these two years of touring with *If My People*? The greatest benefits were the relationships and the unity that was built among us as believers, churches and Christian organizations. Simply getting to know one another enabled us to develop trust across denominational barriers. As we lifted up prayer for these cities and countries, doors began to open for future outreaches together. Loren Cunningham, quoting a pioneer of Christian unity, often stated: "In important issues, unity; in lesser issues, liberty; but in all things, charity."

The following summer of 1978, YWAM was able to kick off their Summer of Service in Chalon-sur-Saône, using the facilities of La Porte Ouverte (The Open Door), a missionary training center. Another great expression of unity followed as teams spread out across France, working with different Christian organizations. This included an outreach called Punch planned by several Christian groups on the beaches of southern France, the Gagnières summer camp, as well as local church outreaches in Normandy and other regions.

During our first tour we had met Yves Brunet, who had opened a recording studio in Reims, France. He invited our team to cut an album (yes, a vinyl record!) of *Si mon peuple*. We were grateful for this collaboration and made the recording in July 1977.[2]

The new style of praise and worship was becoming another unifying factor among believers. At this time the worship movement was still in its early stages. Traveling to so many locations brought a spark of life to the body of Christ and spread the impact of new worship music.

One of my greatest personal joys was meeting French Christian composers. I kept a list of their names and prayed for them. Then when it was time to prepare a new supplement for our songbook, *J'aime l'Eternel*, I would contact them to see if they had new songs that we could publish. This became a precious collaboration and worship resource for French-speaking Christians.

The most rewarding answer to prayer came in 1978 when Alain Schwartz, the pastor at the Reformed Church of Saint-Laurent-du-Pape who had earlier hosted the *Si mon peuple* team, opened the door for thirty young people from YWAM Switzerland to move to France. They were initially housed in the nearby town of Charmes at the Maison de l'Union de Prière.[3] Several from our team moved there to help pioneer this effort. Daniel Schaerer was named the YWAM National Director for France, leading the group as they interceded for a permanent center and for the country. A few months later Daniel was able to negotiate an agreement for his team to move to a former orphanage at Le Gault-la-Forêt, 120 kilometers (80 miles) east of Paris. *Voilà!* YWAM France had been born!

2. *Si mon peuple.* This recording is available on CD in French at www.jem -editions.ch.

3. English: House of the Prayer Union, which is located in a village of the Rhone valley in the middle of France.

Proclamation

"H E I S Lord, He is Lord! He has risen from the dead and He is Lord!" It was 1972, during my School of Evangelism field trip, and this was my first experience with proclamation. We had arrived by bus in Turkey and were visiting the ancient city of Ephesus.

As we walked down the timeworn marble streets flanked by Roman pillars, we observed the ancient ruins and imagined the scenes played out during early Christendom. It was so foreign to me to think that people would worship other gods than the God of the Bible, yet this city had been dedicated to Artemis, the mistress of wild animals and the goddess of hunting and fertility.

We gathered in the large amphitheater of Ephesus and listened to one of our classmates retell the historical happenings of that city. As a concluding note, we raised our voices together to exclaim in song: "He is Lord, He is Lord! He has risen from the dead and He is Lord. Every knee shall bow and every tongue confess that Jesus Christ is Lord!" A ripple of excitement ran through me as I sensed the authority of this truth and the importance of declaring it. Christ's resurrection had proved itself far greater than any other power of that era or of our present day. This was the first time I remember proclaiming His character and His worth in a public place.

YWAM has always fixed a high value on evangelism, going out to meet people where they are and telling them of God's love. "To make God known" is part of our motto. We had been witnessing two-by-two in the streets of cities for a long time, but proclamation through song and dance in large groups was still new to us. The first large outreach we had in Europe was during the Munich 1972 Olympic games. Young people came from all over the world to join YWAM's outreach and bring the message of Christ to the nations gathered there. Then an outbreak of violence in the Olympic village shocked the world: eleven Israeli athletes were taken hostage and then killed by terrorists. In response to this tragedy, a thousand of our young people walked through the streets singing and handing out flowers to the public in an effort to console them.

The following years we focused on witnessing in the cities of Amsterdam, Paris, Montreal and Venice. During Easter vacation of 1979, many YWAMers gathered in Neuchâtel, Switzerland, for ten days of evangelism. I had arranged several songs for a choir and my colleague, Louise, had made costumes for the dancers. Heinz and Jolinette Suter had contacted city authorities, who gave us permission to perform in key locations. I went a few days early with the dance team to check out the places where we would perform and we were doused with rain and snow! How could we even think of taking our instruments outside under these conditions? Two days later, however, as the others arrived, the sun came out and shone brightly the entire time.

As we began the week of outreach, our French ministry leader, Tom Bloomer, declared: "Pour l'amour de Neuchâtel, je ne me tairai point" ("For the love of Neuchâtel, I will not be silent.") As it was Easter week, we went out to the streets to sing and proclaim: "He's alive!" Our goal was to fill this town with the message of Christ's resurrection. YWAM rented the town theater and already the first night the 550-seat auditorium was nearly full. Around twenty people accepted the invitation to give their lives to Christ during that week. It was becoming more natural to proclaim the goodness of God and His kingdom in the public arena.

That summer we were planning an outreach in the city of Avignon, France. Every summer this city hosts a well-known festival, which is a gathering place for artists and tourists from all over Europe. So we challenged Christian young people to join us to witness about their life in Christ during this Summer of Service. It could be difficult to find places to perform, to meet . . . and to sleep! A small team of French YWAMers was already planning the logistics for this outreach. Three of my colleagues and I drove down from Lausanne to "scout out the land" and to prepare in prayer for our performances. I remember intentionally walking over the large open terrace in front of the Palace of the Popes, asking God to reserve it for our evening programs. The marble-covered square would be the perfect place for our dance teams and the backdrop of the palace was absolutely stunning.

Two hundred and sixty of us from 15 different countries converged on Avignon that summer of 1979. We found a campground on the far side of the Rhone River, walking the one kilometer distance to and from this walled city four to six times a day. No, it was not the famous *Pont d'Avignon* from the well-known song. That bridge only goes out 360 feet and stops mid-river!

The local Protestants loaned us their 14th century Reformed church, Temple Saint-Martial, for the entire six weeks of outreach. Yes, six weeks! It was there that we gathered daily for worship, prayer and teaching. Then after a *siesta* we would go out in small teams to meet people on the streets and invite them to the evening performances.

The first week, however, was dedicated to teaching and prayer walks throughout Avignon. We had been warned to expect violence and theft, so we prayed specifically for peace. The police reported after ten days that they were amazed that there was so little crime on the streets. They said: "An unusual peaceful atmosphere reigns here this year." We knew that our prayers and God's presence were bringing the effect of salt and light into the city.

One day we prayed specifically for the media. That same afternoon we met a Catholic journalist who interviewed us and wrote an encouraging review about our activities in the regional newspaper.

That evening, a French television crew showed up to film us. They then broadcasted part of our production on national TV! What amazing answers to our prayers.

At the midpoint of the outreach our leaders began an informal discipleship program for those who had given their lives to Christ, including one young Egyptian man who went on to become a Christian leader in his area of the world. They met each evening at the Protestant church. By the end of the summer the church was full! The last evening ten more individuals gave their hearts to Christ. Our local Christian friends gave us great support all along and promised to follow up the new believers.

In 1980 we returned to Avignon with a street presentation called *l'Ami (The Friend)*.[1] My colleague, Rolf Schneider, and I, along with Sharon, Thierry and Liliane had prayed for weeks over the content of this musical drama. How could we best present God to a non-believer? We were convinced we should try to express the Creator's original intention for friendship with man, followed by His broken heart when man rejected that plan and chose to live without His fellowship. We then wrote a song about God reaching out His arms to a world that no longer knew Him. The street drama ended with an invitation to return to the Father and to receive His life through His Son, Jesus. The theme song, *"Avoir Dieu pour ami"* (*"To have God as a friend"*), expressed the joy of entering into a relationship with Him. We recorded the sound-track in June just in time for the dancers to practice the choreography. Not only was *l'Ami* performed in Avignon, but teams continued to tour with this street musical for several years across Europe and Africa.

Avignon was a magical place during the summer months with the theater festival in full swing and numerous musicians playing throughout the city. Each evening we experienced a very tangible presence of God as our groups performed in front of the Palace of the Popes. One night I met a young woman named Renée, who had been returning regularly. I asked her, "What brings you back here night after night?" She said, "There's such a peace in this place." Renée told us about her struggles as a single mom since her husband had committed suicide. We had already shared the gospel with her and now continued to pray

---

1. The street musical *l'Ami* is available on DVD in French at www.jem-editions.ch.

that God's love would restore her shattered life. Eventually Renée came and visited us in Switzerland. She was just one of so many lonely and hurting people that we met during this outreach.

In 1983 we created another musical drama, *Le Chanteur (The Singer)*[2], for our summer outreach in Avignon. We drew the storyline from a book by the same name, written by Calvin Miller. It is a powerful extended metaphor of Jesus' incarnation and the redemption of man. Working from his text, several of our musicians along with a choreographer created new songs and movement to express the message. Around five hundred people participated in YWAM's outreach that summer, and we performed in three locations daily. Not only did our group enact *Le Chanteur*, but Karen Lafferty brought a team from Amsterdam, Musicians for Missions; Claude Fraysse came with singers from the center of France; and the Trio Roffidal added their beautiful voices to the sounds of Avignon.

The joys of welcoming so many people were accompanied by certain challenges . . . including the 105°F (40°C) weather, the complications of managing several artistic groups, and the tragic accidental death of one of our African participants. However, the gospel was again announced to thousands of visitors and residents of Avignon.

Declaring the truth about God and His character has been a key aspect of learning to worship. There's something very powerful about proclaiming who He is. It establishes faith in our hearts as well as in the hearts of others. David Garratt had taught us: "Truth in the mouth of God's people becomes a weapon to transform cultures." Announcing the Father's love and the person of Jesus Christ publicly to those who don't yet know Him has now become a passion in our lives! What could be more worthy of our efforts?

2. The street drama *Le Chanteur* is available in French on DVD at www.jem-editions.ch.

Burnout

I HAD just been out for a walk in the fragrant forest at Chalet-à-Gobet. The raspberries were ready to pick and I was prepared, bucket in hand. Reaching my bare arms in through the prickly leaves and thorns, I was getting scratched . . . a lot. The berries were beautiful so I couldn't help but reach in through the briars to get the best ones. "Ouch! That hurt." Walking back to my apartment, I reflected: *This is no different than over-stretching my energy while on tour with a YWAM team, or staying up too late talking with friends. In any event, I won! I got my berries.* But to gain the reward I had to suffer the consequences of some nasty scratches.

This experience led me to reflect on my way of living out my ministry. I had achieved most of my goals, but I was paying a heavy price. My body was wearing out long before my heart and spirit were ready to slow down. As I considered all the touring I had done since joining YWAM, I realized that in 1976 alone I had participated in eight different traveling teams. I was stunned! There was no way I could survive as an introvert while living continuously with groups of people in tight quarters. I had not yet understood my need for individual space; I just knew that I felt tired all the time. I wrote a letter to the Lord in May 1976: "Dear Father, I think I need to learn more about You and Your strength and character . . . because I am carrying too many things on my shoulders. Will You help me?" Then in August of that year I added in my journal: "I'm not able to spend every moment, day and night, in ministry."

I remember writing to my parents during the Olympic Outreach in Montreal where seventeen hundred people had gathered in the small town of Dunham, Canada: "At least we have a room to sleep in, even though there are no beds." This had been my third large Summer of Service in four years. I carried huge responsibilities, including caring for a team of twenty-four youth and leading a French choir of thirty singers. I took our group into Montreal every other day, all the while getting little sleep. Immediately afterwards I continued with another team, ministering among the Charismatic Catholics in Quebec. Upon finishing those six weeks of fruitful outreach, although physically drained, I commented in my journal, "This must be a revival! How can I *not* be part of it?" I so desired to move ahead, but inside of me, my body and soul were screaming: *I can't do this any longer!*

Earlier that year I had traveled for five weeks with a music team which accompanied a multi-media presentation. We had performed in 24 cities all over French-speaking Europe. It was an effective team, but the rigors of travel and constant people contact were a strain, even though we planned regular days of rest.

Then there was the trip to Hurlach that spring with four co-workers to make corrections on the supplement to our songbook. Upon my return to Lausanne, I had rehearsed with a choir and recorded an album. No wonder my blood pressure was high! No wonder I felt tired and overwhelmed at times, but I could not read the signs. Burnout was not yet a concept that we understood in YWAM.

This pace continued the following year with some exciting opportunities to create the musical, *Si mon peuple* (*If My People*), and to tour with the team. Despite my fatigue, I would not have traded these experiences for anything! We saw God at work bringing praise to His name and bringing unity to His people throughout French-speaking Europe.

I also continued participating in other YWAM outreaches, one in particular was to Venice for two months in 1978. Several hundred of us YWAMers were camping there. Change was constant. We had expected to go to Argentina from Venice to join their outreach via the *Anastasis*,[1] a ship YWAM was just purchasing and had started renovating. But that trip was not to be. Misevaluating the extensive work that needed to be done before we could sail, our leaders made a "plan B." Teams went out to Spain, Turkey, ex-Yugoslavia, and other Mediterranean countries to share about Christ. I stayed in Venice to lead a small team of women who visited the poor and helped in Catholic children's' camps.

I would often take my guitar and sing with the kids. One day I found it difficult to connect with them, so I decided I needed to fast and pray more, eating only one meal a day. A week later I was sick and the doctor on-site said: "REST!" However, I was scheduled to leave for Switzerland two days later and go directly to the French Summer of Service. On arrival, my French co-workers saw that I was not well. So after two weeks of leading worship and participating in the training, they helped me organize a time of rest at a friend's home in the Swiss Alps. Forced rest. I didn't know how to do it for myself.

I had been sleeping poorly for some time and even after two weeks off I was still not sleeping well. Once again, my leaders were attentive to my needs and we prayed about better long-term housing. They found an apartment just down the street from our center and suggested that I move into it with three other women. I was so excited. I had moved so many times, leaving my room to others while I was on tour, with my affairs stored in the attic of YWAM Chalet-à-Gobet. I had slept in almost every room in the building! That night I carried my sleeping bag and air mattress down the street to my new apartment and slept on the floor. We didn't have any furniture yet, but it didn't matter. At last, I had a place to call home and leave my things in a room . . . and a kitchen! I love to cook, but up to that time I had always eaten in the community dining room. It made me feel like a queen in her palace to have my own home and my own kitchen. And even though I needed to be off again for another *Si mon peuple* tour in October of 1978, I could look forward to a quiet place upon my return, two and a half months later.

1. The M/V *Anastasis* was the first ship launched by Mercy Ships.

Living with constant fatigue, I sometimes felt there was no hope for the future. I held on tightly, however, to the promise in John 15 that if I abide in Christ and He in me, I would bear much fruit and the Father would be glorified. As the years went by, I had the privilege of seeing some of the fruit of our ministry. Yet at times I found myself serving without my heart being in it. One of my well-meaning colleagues confronted me about this, thinking it was an attitude problem. This only added to my pressure and fatigue. I honestly didn't know what to do differently to get in touch with my heart and I couldn't imagine not continuing to serve the Lord. I read A. W. Tozer's inspiring book that describes faith as "the gaze of a soul upon a saving God."[2] Although this helped me to practice His presence and to rest in Him, the reality was that my body and my emotions were wearing out and it was affecting my behavior.

Another aspect of my fatigue was relational. Many of my friends in YWAM had married. I had arranged special music, directed choirs and played for dozens of weddings, but I was still waiting for Mr. Right to come along. At different times I had prayed about this subject and felt assured that I would get married one day. Towards the end of 1976 I had begun a friendship with a young Frenchman who also loved music. However, in the spring of 1978, after counseling with our YWAM leaders, we understood that our relationship should not go any further than friendship. So this left me lonely and wondering if I would ever experience the joy of marriage. As I prayed that summer, one specific verse from the Old Testament stood out to me saying that the Israelites should not marry a foreigner (Deuteronomy 7:3). *Could this be God's wisdom for my choice of a husband?* I wondered. *Would God bring a man into my life from my own country?* Only time would tell, but I started to understand my need for ongoing friendships, whether or not I got married. I have many wonderful friends within YWAM, but I also found it important to develop relationships outside of our organization, as YWAMers are often very mobile, frequently moving on to new mission fields.

My exhaustion came to a head as I was serving as music director for

2. A. W. Tozer, *The Pursuit of God* (Camp Hill, PA: Christian Publications, 1982), 89.

Mission '80 in Lausanne.[3] It was a fabulous opportunity as thousands were coming together at the end of 1979 to hear about missions and to see in the New Year. I had been meeting with musicians, worship leaders and staff for the event since the beginning of the year. I had already recruited many people and was inviting local choirs to form one large group for the event. Greater audience participation in worship had become a high priority for Christian gatherings, so I was preparing a forty-song booklet in three languages (English, French, and German), with a words-only version in still six more languages! It was a huge undertaking, especially remembering that computer music programs and internet communication did not yet exist.

One month before the event, the number of young people registered to attend practically doubled overnight. To accommodate these seven thousand people, a decision was made to run two programs simultaneously. So now we would need twice the number of worship leaders! Gratefully, in spite of the short notice, I was able to recruit a YWAM worship leader from Austria, Bruce Clewett, who came with a team to lead in German. Doubling the program meant a heavier schedule not only for us, but for all of our musicians. Anne-Marie Bossy, a Swiss theological student, accepted to be my assistant. Neither she nor I knew at the time that she would end up running the show and I would spend many hours lying crumpled on a mattress in my office, just trying to be present to cover the essentials. I saved what little strength I had left to go down and direct the choir for the plenary sessions. The event was spectacular for the kingdom of God and the recruiting of young missionaries. But I was totally spent and exhausted, having seriously overstepped my physical and emotional limits. Even after six weeks of rest at my parents' home in early 1980, I was still not able to regain my strength.

By April of 1980 I wanted to resume some ministry involvement. I started with our Easter outreach. This time we were targeting the city of Nyon, Switzerland. With the help of our music team I prepared a choir to sing for the large gatherings each evening in the high school

---

3. Mission '80, organized by The European Missionary Association (TEMA), was a large missions conference held in Lausanne to recruit European youth into missions.

auditorium. Heinz and Jolinette Suter and the YWAMers from Burtigny[4] were organizing the event. Over two hundred young people joined us as we went door-to-door during the day to homes and to the hospital, sharing our testimonies, literature and songs. Almost every church in the city participated in this effort. It is such a wonderful experience when believers come together to reach a city.

In September, I lived out a huge turning point in my life. Our French-speaking staff had gathered for a retreat at Burtigny in Switzerland. There were 150 of us working full-time with YWAM. On the way to the retreat, our French YWAM director talked with me about passing on the leadership baton of the music ministry to my co-worker Rolf Schneider. Many had noticed my downslide in health. Also, we were about to start a yearlong music team, in which Rolf would lead and I would participate, along with six other people. So it seemed like a logical step, but I couldn't grasp how I could continue without having some kind of leadership role in the ministry I had pioneered.

I took a walk to the little church in Burtigny to have time to think and pray. "God, they are asking me to give up *my baby*! What should I do?" It was a difficult decision, since I had given myself so completely to build this ministry. It had corresponded to the call of God on my life. I couldn't see myself doing anything else or going anywhere else, although my strength and stamina were failing. As I sat in tears, I sensed God answered me: "They are asking you to let your child be adopted by another couple." . . . *My child?* I questioned. Yes, the French songbook was no longer a baby but a growing child. *Adopted? What does that mean? Am I an unfit mother? Would I have to give up all my rights to see my child? To train it? Would I have a say in the decisions that would be made for the future of this ministry? How can I stay in this work and simply be a follower?*

I had worked often with Rolf and Maryse Schneider. I had great confidence in them and their commitment to God and to music ministry. I knew they respected me and cared for me, but I still couldn't figure out how this arrangement would work. YWAM did not have a

4. Burtigny is a small village just above Gland, Switzerland. From 1979, Heinz and Jolinette Suter, with the help of a team, developed a former orphanage into a YWAM training center.

precedent of an older leader staying when a younger leader stepped in. We prayed together with the ministry leaders at the retreat and they *all* agreed it was time for Rolf to take over. What a shock! I felt all alone and set aside like an old rag, although I couldn't express it at the time.

Thankfully our leaders waited to make this decision public until I was at peace with it. A few weeks later, I proposed a "marriage of ministries" between Rolf and Maryse and me. Rolf would take over the general direction of the ministry and the administration, while I would take time to compose, to teach and would still have a voice in future decisions. The others seemed to be in agreement with this. So in October we announced this new phase of the YWAM French Music Ministry. As a result of this decision, it was like a load was lifted from my shoulders. I no longer felt the obligation to serve every time someone needed a musician, although it was still uncomfortable for me to let go and not be involved in every decision as in the past.

As the new music team came together in the fall of 1980, we continued to process how to proceed in this new format. Rolf and Maryse, Sharon and Michel, Serge, Thierry, Catherine, Lisette, Jean-Luc, and I met daily to practice and prepare different performances. We were living in the farm village of Burtigny at the new YWAM center. Not only did we write music, but we also picked and sorted potatoes together, washed dishes, shoveled snow and made a fire each morning in the potbelly stove. In January 1981, a couple of them helped me complete a fifty-song addition, *Qui est semblable à toi?* (*Who is like unto You?*), to our songbook.

In February, we organized a bilingual music seminar for the first time. Over two hundred of our musician friends and YWAMers gathered to hear David and Dale Garratt, our worship mentors from New Zealand. At that time David prophesied over our music ministry: "God wants to put several of you together to form a strong arrow that can be shot anywhere to minister, even across cultures." This helped confirm to me the commitment we had made to work together. We were already seeing our ministry strengthened as we harmonized our gifts and efforts.

That year our team led worship for sixty-eight meetings, touching around 13,700 people and participating in both the Easter and summer

YWAM outreaches to the city of Geneva. We made two recordings, *L'Ami* and *Pour nous un Père*.[5] One very unique invitation came to our team from Nîmes, France, where we were invited to sing for La Fête de l'Evangile (The Festival of the Gospel) in the Roman arena with fifteen thousand Christians celebrating the event! I also had the privilege of teaching and leading worship at two music seminars in the south of France for the Assemblies of God church musicians, organized by our good friend, Joseph Broussaudier. The icing on the cake came that fall when God gave us a full-time secretary, Jocelyne Muller. What a gift! She would carry the load of organizing our ministry and become a great friend.

Yet even with a team around me, I was burning out again. I had never imagined that I could burn out doing the things I loved. But God places His life in earthen vessels that can be broken. I continued another two years in relatively productive ministry, though my strength was limited and my health was still going downhill. In December 1983 I returned to the States to care for my ongoing physical problems, not knowing what my future would hold. It looked like this chapter of my life was closing. Thankfully God had provided others who would carry on YWAM's French Music Ministry.

This meditation by Ruskin was a great inspiration for me:

There is no music in a "rest," but there is the making of music in it. In our whole life-melody the music is broken off here and there by "rest" and we foolishly think we have come to the end of the tune. God sends a time of forced leisure, sickness, disappointed plans, frustrated efforts, and makes a sudden pause in the choral hymn of our lives: and we lament that our voices must be silent, and our part missing in the music which ever goes up to the ear of the Creator.

How does the musician read the "rest"? See him beat the time with unvarying count, and catch up the next note true and steady, as if no breaking place had come between.

Not without design does God write the music of our lives. Be it's ours to learn the tune, and not be dismayed at the "rest." They

5. English: *A Father for us.* This recording is available in French on volumes 1–3 of the CD series *Pour le louer* at www.jem-editions.ch.

are not to be slurred over, not to be omitted, not to destroy the melody, not to change the keynote.

If we look up, God Himself will beat the time for us. With the eye on Him, we shall strike the next note full and clear. If we sadly say to ourselves, "There is no music in a 'rest,'" let us not forget: there is the making of music in it. The making of music is often a slow and painful process in this life. How patiently God works to teach us![6]

---

6. Taken from *Streams in the Desert*, compiled by Mrs. Charles E. Cowman (Grand Rapids: Zondervan, 1984).

ELEVEN

Restoration

"NOW I will arise," says the LORD; "I will set him in the safety for which he longs" (Psalm 12:5). This psalm intrigued me. What was God telling me at the beginning of this new year? Would I have better financial support? Or was there a deeper meaning at this broken time in my life? As 1984 unfolded, I realized it meant much more than financial security. Before returning to the United States I had asked God for total restoration: renewal of my body, my soul, my mind and my spirit.

Once I arrived in Iowa, I saw a doctor who put me through a series of tests and diagnosed my physical condition as "burn-out" and Irritable Bowel Syndrome. Within weeks a simple medication helped regulate my digestive system, but I still needed to learn to live a more restful lifestyle. Living with my parents for several months helped me to curb my travel and to relax. However, in our rural farm culture, everybody works hard. They thought that if I was going to stay for a while, I should be looking for a job, even if only part-time. My doctor was very helpful in this situation. He told me in the presence of my parents that I should not be obliged to do everything they do. His wise input helped us all to lower our expectations, so I did not look for a job.

I was considering taking a year to study, and I kept running across bumper stickers from Wheaton College. *Is God trying to direct me there to take classes?* I wondered. What an innovative way for Him to speak to me! Knowing that they have a fabulous Conservatory of Music, I started investigating this avenue and was able to qualify for financial aid for one semester. I was accepted, and at the age of thirty-four became an undergraduate student once again. Learning is an ongoing love of mine. Being able to study and to write in my mother tongue was a piece of cake, especially after doing everything in French for over twelve years. It was such a renewing process for me and nourished my mind and my soul. This was certainly part of God's answer to my prayer for restoration.

My advisor at Wheaton couldn't believe I wanted to take eighteen hours of classes a week. He didn't understand that missionaries want to get the most for their money! In reality, I still had not learned to slow down. I studied advanced music theory, orchestration, different music cultures from around the world, business French, biculturalism and took piano and voice lessons. Several times a month there were free concerts for students so I attended many of them.

During my class on biculturalism, I heard for the first time about "culture shock" and the phases in adapting as a foreigner. I had walked through many cross-cultural experiences without understanding the emotional pressures of adjusting to a new country. It was healing to my heart to know that certain reactions are normal when you live in a second culture. For example, I had often felt inadequate because of my limited French. In the beginning I spoke like a novice, making many mistakes and needing the help of others in order to speak correctly. Writing in French was very time consuming and always needed to be reviewed by a co-worker. This made it so slow to achieve anything and increased the frustration of communicating.

In the area of relationships on the mission field, I had chosen to make friends primarily with the French-speakers because of God's call on my life. I rarely took time to be with English speakers, although I realized it was refreshing when I did. Now it was clear that I had neglected my own roots as an American and needed to give myself greater freedom to form friendships within my own language and cultural group.

On campus I was able to meet some missionaries who were studying in the graduate program at Wheaton College and sat in on one of their luncheons. The speaker was from the psychology department, Dr. Fran White. She advised us not only to use our time for studies while in Wheaton but to take time for relationships. I thought: *No way! I just want to learn everything I can and get back to Europe.* Wrong! I really needed and desired deep relationships with others. I also welcomed the thought of finding a husband, but that was not my goal in coming to Wheaton. In fact, I had somewhat given up on marriage.

Nonetheless, while having lunch one day with a group of French-speaking students in the cafeteria, a young man happened to be sitting at our table and seemed to be listening to our conversation. He finally acknowledged that he spoke French, but only after everyone else had left the table.

He said to me, "*Votre prononciation est très bonne, mademoiselle.*" ("Miss, your pronunciation is very good.") My inkling being confirmed that he had understood our conversation, I shot back several questions: "*Je pensais bien que vous compreniez le français! Qu'est-ce que vous étudiez ici?*" ("I thought you understood French! What are you studying here?") He responded to me in a very strange language. Bewildered, I looked at him and said in English: "So where do you come from?" Realizing that he had just answered me in Japanese, he apologized for mixing up the languages. He explained that he had just returned from a three-year mission term in Japan and was here studying in Wheaton's graduate program for Missions and Intercultural Studies. His name was Tom Panci.

Tom explained more to me about the master's program, which was designed for missionaries on furlough. He said that perhaps I could qualify to receive a grant, enabling me to earn a master's degree after fourteen months of studies. He asked for my phone number and added, "As the chairman of the Graduate Missionary Students' Fellowship on campus, it is my responsibility to keep in touch with everyone." I thought, *My phone number?*

The following semester, January 1985, I did receive a grant from the Hermann Fund, enabling me to continue my studies at Wheaton, but now as a graduate student. During classes I kept running into Tom. In one course, called "Participant Observation,"[1] we were asked to make a list of fifty ideas for a cultural observation project. I chose the first option on my list, Wheaton College undergraduate chapel services. I wanted to analyze what was valid in worship for the younger generation in America. Tom, sitting a few rows behind me, was talking with another student about his choice of topic, the last one on his list. Bingo . . . the same as mine! I turned around and said, "Tom Panci, you stole my project!" The professor had encouraged us to work with each other if we found someone observing the same domain. So the next day Tom asked me if we could do the assignment together. I wondered if it was wise to spend that much time with this friendly young man, but I finally accepted.

My emotions were still fragile. Actually, I should say, my *lack* of emotions. I hadn't felt much of anything for months, except for feeling disoriented, having left the mission field. Maybe I was afraid of feeling something again. Besides, the hope of returning to Europe still lived in my heart, along with the fear that if I got attached to someone here, it would be more painful to leave. However, Tom made me comfortable with his easy-going way and warm spirit. Within a few weeks of seeing each other regularly during classes and for this observation project, we both began looking forward to those moments together. He was fun to be with and he made me laugh. I started to feel like a real person again, not just an empty shell.

As our relationship grew, I reminded Tom that my call was to the French-speaking world and if he had hopes of going back to Japan or elsewhere, we shouldn't allow our friendship to go deeper. That was a hard thing for me to say and for him to hear. He was, however, quite open to going to a different country; plus he had studied French for six years. Tom was also convinced that he did not want go back to the mission field without a wife!

As we talked and prayed during that semester, Tom challenged me to detach myself from my past ministry if I wanted to let our relationship

1. This course consists of learning through observation and participation in a cultural situation.

grow. It was one of the hardest things I ever did. I had loved my job and had spent twelve and a half years following my passion and call to develop French Christian music. Yes, as Tom had noticed I was very work-oriented, but marriage would need to take a higher priority than my profession. *Perhaps this deepening friendship with him would bring more balance into my life?* Already my emotions and hope were being restored.

That spring I went to meet my friends from the French Music Ministry who were touring in Quebec. I invited Tom to join us for a short stay. I wanted to know what they thought about my boyfriend. The first night I sat down with my friend, Jocelyne, and we hashed out my list of pros and cons for this relationship. I needed to make a decision. Tom had already told me that if he were to ask me to marry him, he wanted me to be ready to set aside my previous ministry and be open to whatever God had for us as a couple. This was a tough step for me. In those few days together, Tom won the hearts of my colleagues . . . as he had already won mine.

On July 14, the French National holiday, we were back in Wheaton, sitting on a park bench in a beautiful petunia garden at Cantigny Park, when Tom asked me to marry him! He had just returned from a secret trip to Iowa to visit my parents and ask for my hand in marriage. We had been to an evening church service where a music group had sung a song written to Psalm 34:3, "Let us exalt His name together, forever." What I didn't know was that he had chosen this exact verse years ago in praying for his future wife. For Tom, it was a real confirmation of his choice to propose to me that night.

I made him wait two weeks for my answer. I was in the middle of an intensive class at the time and was still in the process of laying down my past ministry. I needed time to let it go and feel assured that this was God's will, before I could enter into the joy of this decision. When I told him "yes," it was after making him his favorite supper, bacon and eggs, and washing his feet as Jesus had done for his disciples, as an expression of my love. I looked into his eyes and said: "Tom, I want to be your helper."

We were married on December 31, 1985, in a red brick church with beautiful stained glass windows in my hometown of Newton, Iowa.

Tom's parents along with his two brothers and sister were able to come from Detroit, Michigan and our two families enjoyed getting to know each other. Both my YWAM director, Tom Bloomer, and Tom's spiritual dad, Jerry Erdmann, brought messages for the celebration, with the pastor of my little country church in Metz, Harold Den Hartog, presiding. My two best friends from Europe, Cynthia Bloomer and Jocelyne Muller, came as bridesmaids.

We made our home initially in Wheaton, Illinois, as we completed our studies for our master's degrees, graduating in May of 1986. Tom suggested that we take a year to really get to know each other and not jump back onto the mission field right away. He worked at Scripture Press, a Christian publishing company, and I was employed as a secretary for International Christian Fellowship. We joined a very friendly, relationally-oriented church, Wheaton Wesleyan, and appreciated living close enough to the Wheaton College campus to attend some of their activities.

God's plans are so good. I have greatly enjoyed Tom's presence, his kindness, his wisdom and his love. We share many common values on life, family, and missions' perspectives. I felt myself growing stronger physically and emotionally. I could be fulfilled without carrying big projects on my shoulders. God had truly put me "in the safety for which I longed" and it had everything to do with relationship!

TWELVE

Bearing Fruit in Suffering

AFTER much prayer and reflection, Tom and I chose to move to Lausanne, Switzerland, in February 1988 to work with YWAM. Upon arrival at Chalet-à-Gobet, we attended a three-month, bilingual Biblical Counseling School, which laid some good foundations in our hearts for future ministry. To sharpen his language skills, Tom then studied French at the University of Lausanne for two semesters, and in the summer of 1989 he helped Joe Portale staff a Crossroads DTS.[1]

Two unexpected factors, however, took us by surprise. First, YWAM had recently founded the University of the Nations[2] and the focus of our center at Chalet-à-Gobet was shifting from French Ministries to international training. This change did not exclude French Ministries,

1. The Crossroads Discipleship Training School is a six-month missionary training course designed for people over thirty-five years of age.
2. The University of the Nations (UofN) is YWAM's modular, missions university, offering courses in 160 nations, 97 languages, and 600 training centers, equipping students spiritually, culturally, intellectually, and professionally to use their giftings to communicate the gospel (www.uofn.edu).

however, it carried a greater emphasis on university courses. To make more space for students, our French-speaking ministries and colleagues began moving off campus to other working locations. A series of leadership changes, several due to medical issues, also complicated the situation. We were still fully expecting to get involved with YWAM's French Ministries and to be a link with the local churches. Since this aspect of ministry was starting to decline at our Lausanne center, however, we struggled to understand how we could best serve there.

Tom eventually accepted a position as Personnel Director in the fall of 1989, serving one hundred staff and volunteers. He also took on a role as Assistant Director of Public Relations. I helped by organizing and leading our on-campus worship times. On Sundays we took time to visit the churches of the city and continued to look for opportunities to work with them.

Then came the second surprise . . . a flood of painful emotions engulfed me almost every time I was in contact with the French Music Ministry team. I had been expecting to have great joy to be reunited with these friends and colleagues with whom I had labored to build this ministry. Instead sadness came over me, even though I could see the team growing and each one going forward in his respective gifting. Rolf Schneider and Philippe Bogdan had formed a band called Visa. Later Christine and François Reymond joined their great voices and talents to this group. They traveled often, performing in cafés, prisons, festivals and church events. Jocelyne Muller continued faithfully at her post as the administrative coordinator for the team. Sylvain and Line Freymond linked up with them in 1990 and developed "live" praise recordings and a long-term ministry in leading worship and training worship leaders. David Durham, a gifted composer and performer, joined the team along with his family, adding greater quality to our YWAM productions. So why could I not rejoice more over these developments?

I discovered that the Music Ministry had a new mode of operating, with each member forming his own team. In the past we had all worked together on each other's projects. I was uncomfortable with this new format and struggled to find my place. I was also torn because I desired to work more closely with Tom. I considered the option of staffing one of YWAM's UofN schools, but because of my experiences with burnout,

I was hesitant to take on such an intense schedule. It was becoming painfully obvious that I needed a new field to plow.

A door of opportunity opened for me to teach several hours a week at a Christian music school, Psalmodia,[3] started by Guy Barblan in 1989, near Lausanne. I had always desired to be a part of a center that was set aside for the on-going training of musicians and the promotion of musical performances. In former years at YWAM, the only piano was in the main classroom so I had to schedule every free moment of the day in order to get one hour on the piano. The opening of Psalmodia was a dream come true . . . six pianos under one roof! I was able to walk in as a piano teacher and choir director without having the headaches of practical organization. I was so thankful.

Although our involvements had become more defined, Tom and I found our path strewn with landmines. After only a couple of years serving as Personnel Director and other leadership roles, Tom became overwhelmed with the administrative duties and relational conflicts needing resolution. Now it was his turn to come face-to-face with burnout. Tom's gifts lie in personal contacts and discipleship, but most of his energy was being funneled into office and management work. In 1993 the Swiss authorities were requiring that our main building be closed down for some necessary building renovations, in particular the installation of a high-tech fire alarm system. The small leadership team could not come to an agreement about how to handle the situation. Tom was a part of that team and the stress of the unresolved conflict was crushing him. I had never seen him depressed before that time.

I had my own challenges to face as well. My life's calling was to lead worship and provide worship materials for French-speaking believers. But every time I attended a worship event where my Music Ministry colleagues were leading, I would cry. I couldn't identify the source of my pain, but obviously I was grieving over some sort of loss. In my head I understood that situations change and life moves on, but my heart and even my body were telling me that something was wrong.

My health had been going downhill inexplicably for months, then my intestinal pain increased to the point that I had to be hospitalized in January 1992. I was diagnosed with Crohn's disease, an autoimmune

3. www.psalmodia.net

condition with inflammation of the large bowel. The doctor decided not to operate. I was treated for five weeks with cortisone, antibiotics and a feeding tube until I could be stabilized. Finally I was able to return home, but the cortisone treatment continued for months, so I was very weak. Tom became chief cook, house-cleaner and nurse as well as assuming his work at YWAM. This was not my idea of a ministry together.

Then in November 1992, Tom's mother passed away suddenly, adding to our stress. We made a quick trip to the States. Thankfully Tom's brothers and sister have tight relationships, so they were able to help each other and their father through this time of grief. Tom's cup of adversity, however, was full to overflowing.

In May 1993, he resigned from the leadership team, but continued to serve as Personnel and Public Relations Director at YWAM Lausanne. Many colleagues had left with only twenty-five people remaining on staff. Tom was at the end of his strength, but because of loyalty, he would not permit himself to be released from his administrative responsibilities. Two of our Swiss leaders, Eliane Lack and Heinz Suter, realized that Tom was on the edge of a nervous breakdown and stepped in to shoulder the crisis, freeing him from his work. The Lausanne campus was closed down for a year, the building totally gutted and eventually rebuilt.

In June, I had a second attack of Crohn's disease so Tom again took on all the household jobs. My convalescence lasted for almost nine months. We asked God if He was trying to tell us something. *Do we need to leave YWAM? And Switzerland?* We asked our supporting churches in the States to pray for us. Two of them responded with an invitation to come back and rest. We accepted. Wheaton Wesleyan Church in Illinois rented us an apartment near them for the month of July 1994. Afterwards, Trinity Church welcomed us to Lansing, Michigan, where we stayed in an apartment of a member's home, received medical care and plugged into their mission's department for four months.

The mission's director at Trinity wanted us to meet David and Aletha Kuenstler, both psychiatric nurses, who attended the church. Aletha also had Crohn's disease, among a dozen other chronic illnesses.[4]

4. Aletha Kuenstler has written a book on dealing with chronic illness: *Chronic Illness: Facing Its Challenges* (Xulon, 2011), www.chronicillnessfacingitschallenges.com.

I remember our first Sunday back at Trinity, a church of around nine hundred people at the time. A couple came in and sat down beside us just as the service was beginning. I was convinced that this was the couple who we were supposed to meet. I had never seen a photograph of them, but somehow, I knew. When the service ended, the lady leaned over and introduced herself. It was Aletha! God led her right to me. She became my mentor for learning to live with a chronic illness, talking me through the symptoms and treatments. I have seldom met a person who has such a positive approach to life. She taught me to *live* again. Tom equally appreciated David and was able to walk through the reasons for his burnout. This was an incredible provision for our emotional and physical restoration, and a deep friendship has continued with this very unique couple.

As life and strength seeped back into our beings we began to dream again. One day I was out for a prayer walk and a new thought sprang into my mind. When I returned to the apartment I said to Tom: "Why don't we research the names of God and dig deeper into His character to help us get through this tough time?"

Tom had been struggling with depression for over a year. For the first time in months I saw him get excited about something. He responded: "There's nothing I would like better!" Tom loves to study the Bible, so we started researching the different descriptions of God through His Old Testament names. Our hearts gained courage as we wrote down our findings and realized that this could be helpful for other people going through difficult times. We imagined what it would look like to publish this as a book. Maybe God wasn't finished with us yet!

When we returned to Europe in February 1995, we were still facing two unresolved issues. Would a change of location be necessary for Tom to be better placed in using his gifts or would it be sufficient to redefine his role? And what about my continuing emotional pain concerning the Music Ministry? We cried out to God for guidance.

Tom's transition came first. Upon returning, his job description was defined as only Public Relations, with another colleague shouldering the administrative tasks in Personnel. This gave us more time to serve as needed links between YWAM Lausanne and local French-speaking ministries and churches, as we had always desired. Tom was already serving on the organizational team for our YWAM worship celebrations at the Palais de Beaulieu[5] twice every month. We had both been meeting regularly with the pastors of the city through the ACEL committee,[6] and were involved in their joint evangelism efforts and leading Concerts of Prayer. For six years Tom had also led a group of young Chinese restaurant workers in Bible study each Wednesday. What a joy it has been to watch these friends grow and become, in 2008, the Chinese Church of Lausanne, flying with their own wings.[7]

My dilemma finally came to a head one day while I was with a friend who had been with YWAM in the early 1980s. When he questioned me about how I had lived out the change from leading the Music Ministry to simply being a participant, I started to cry. His question had touched an area deep inside me that I had not visited for a long time. It unlocked a door to my true feelings. Earlier I had not been able to admit how hurt I felt at the time of that transition, but now the buried painful experience was screaming for attention. My husband, Tom, encouraged me to ask for help.

Two of my counselor friends helped me to face the feelings of rejection and loss of worth because of reduced ministry responsibilities fifteen years earlier. I began to acknowledge my hidden feelings that had held me captive. I was stuck in a performance orientation, feeling valuable only when I was active in my service for God. I also struggled with an unquenchable need *to belong*. I had a tendency to overextend my physical and emotional limits in order to assure my place in the ministry. No wonder I ended up more than once in burnout!

Experiencing illness had already forced me to look at some of these areas, gaining insight on God's acceptance of me when I could "do" nothing. God was so very present in those dark days of sickness, loving me and reassuring me that my biggest reason for living was "to relate" to Him and others and not just "to serve" Him. Having a husband who

5. Palais de Beaulieu is a conference center in downtown Lausanne where the first International Congress on World Evangelization was held in 1974. YWAM held Sunday evening praise gatherings there for ten years with as many as nine hundred people attending.

6. The Action Commune d'Eglises Lausannoises is an evangelical pastors' committee in the city of Lausanne, a local chapter of the Evangelical Alliance.

7. Gordon and Bei Kan and a team of Chinese elders lead this church.

loved me and valued me even when I was bedridden had helped me to believe in my worth as a person.

During several sessions, my counselors walked me through some painful memories that shook me to the core. They prayed over my brokenness and we worked together to establish truth in my inner being. My healing was not automatic, but took months and years of learning to think differently . . . of replacing wrong thoughts with the truth. I now started with the assumption that *I am valued by my ministry colleagues*, regardless of a defined role or certain limitations.

One day, a good friend, Elsbeth Paterson, drew an illustration for me with three circles. The biggest one was "Linda." Two smaller circles slightly overlapped with mine, one being the Music Ministry and the other being YWAM Lausanne. Neither totally engulfed my circle, underscoring my freedom to be involved in many other areas. Embracing this revelation, I realized that my life consisted not only of what I lived out in YWAM, but that I had space to be myself and to be free to live my dreams beyond this framework.

One important step I needed to take was to officially leave the Music Ministry, though still be a part of YWAM. The former ties had been deeply embedded, but I needed to let them go. Ministries belong to God and not to us. I finally understood that I would always be the "mother" of this work. I did not have to be directly connected with their activities to live out my calling and influence.

I was already working with the Psalmodia music school and was enjoying teaching there. The Forum de Louange (Praise Forum) had also become a vital fellowship link for me. This group of friends, whose main ministries are leading worship and teaching music, represent several Christian organizations and churches. We have met regularly since 1989, to cultivate our relationships, to pray for each other and to promote worship events and discipleship throughout the French-speaking part of Switzerland.

Tom and I did end up leaving the YWAM center at Chalet-à-Gobet. We plugged into YWAM Burtigny, which had a greater involvement in local French-speaking ministries and French publications. In 1998, six years after my debilitating Crohn's attack, we led a bilingual Crossroads DTS there. It was a rewarding experience to walk alongside students and see God transform their lives. Tom also began leading Alpha Courses[8] in collaboration with local churches. Still today, this is one of his greatest joys in ministry, accompanying people who are searching for God. After running fifteen Alpha Courses, we have a large number of "spiritual kids" and cheer them on through the ups and downs of life.

As for the studies that Tom and I had begun on the names of God . . . they had gotten pushed to a back burner, with other things taking precedence. Then, sitting in our church one Sunday morning, Eugene May, a guest speaker, spoke out a prophecy over us as a couple. He knew nothing about us or of our book project. "Don't ever stop writing," he started. "The production of your life is being used to tear down walls of indifference or walls that say: *we can't*. But that which is written by you will say: *we can*, because you did it. I have put the ability in you . . . Write it, write it, write it!" What a confirmation! I was in tears as his words touched me deeply and Tom understood that we really needed to make the writing of this book a priority.

Soon after this, a friend and colleague, Catherine Froehlich, came alongside us to help with the rewrites and the preparation for publishing. Four other French composers joined us, picking up their pens to write of their experiences with our infinite God. Henri-Léon Vaucher, a Swiss professor living in Israel, kindly assisted us as a biblical and Jewish cultural scholar. The book came off the press just before Christmas 1997. We titled it *J'aime ton Nom* (I Love Your Name).[9]

I began composing songs using the names of God in Hebrew that we had described in our book. Discovering His numerous character traits helped me to deepen my heart relationship with God. We found that worship leaders all over the globe were re-centering their attention on God's nature and person in an effort to get back to the heart of worship.

A few years later, Rolf Schneider proposed to me that YWAM produce a solo CD of my new songs. I wondered if I was healed enough from past ministry wounds to carry out such a project. One step at

8. The Alpha Course is a twelve-week series of supper-discussions on knowing God and the Bible. It originated in the Anglican Church of England, was translated into French in 1997, and was launched in French-speaking Switzerland by YWAM.
9. Available in French at www.jem-editions.ch.

a time, I rediscovered the joy of collaborating with my YWAM colleagues. In 2003 we recorded the CD, also entitled *J'aime ton Nom*.[10] I felt restored and affirmed in my inner being by this experience. I could sing the words of my song, "I am not forgotten, for You are El-Roi" (the God who sees), and believe in His acceptance and approval, regardless of my reduced activities.

Learning to love God through life's successes and sufferings has been an apprenticeship for me. In the beginning I only knew that God wanted me to go to France and write songs for Him. There were many hills to climb and some breathtaking mountaintops to visit, but there were also some dark valleys to stumble through. I look back with great thankfulness to God for YWAM and many friends who walked alongside me, as well as the incredible yield of fruit that He gave. Throughout my years of ministry, the verse penned by the Apostle Paul has assured my heart of God's role therein: "But we have this treasure in earthen vessels, so that the surpassing greatness of the power will be of God and not from ourselves" (2 Corinthians 4:7).

As I reflect on the important stepping-stones during my journey in worshiping and loving God, these are the key ones:

- *Knowing God*: the foundation stone in our relationship with Him. Nothing is more important than keeping God and His character at the center of our attention.
- *Singing Scripture*: continually writing new songs that proclaim God's Word and makes it relevant for today.
- *Singing to God*: connecting with the Almighty and pursuing Him in our hearts, while making our songs a prayer and a statement about His goodness and His glory.
- *Thinking God's thoughts*: believing in and acting on His inspiration for my life and ministry.
- *Working in teams*: partnering to maximize our talents and to build His kingdom.
- *Speaking out prophetically*: proclaiming who God is to our world.
- *Trusting God* in suffering and pain.

10. Available in French at JEM Editions (www.jem-editions.ch).

- *Persevering* when things are difficult.

Loving God is more than a special feeling or simply singing songs to Him. It is bowing before Him, acknowledging that He is God in all the circumstances of our lives, whether waiting for the refreshing water of His Spirit after a dry spell or living in the joy of His overflowing abundance. Loving God is a commitment to His person and to fulfill His purposes throughout our lives.

My desire is that each one who reads this book may continue to know God better, to love God more, and to spread His presence throughout the earth.

The Beginning of a Vocation

T H E entire youth group had waited expectantly for this evening to arrive. Despite the gray smoke and charcoal-colored rivers in the mining region of Forbach, France, where I grew up, we often had visitors. This wasn't the Côte d'Azure (French Rivièra), but passing guests had learned to marvel at the tall forests and vast meadows dotted with ponds, which took on the setting of a fantasy film under the foggy haze of winter. The men of this area were rough and black-faced from working in the mines, but had big hearts.

I had come to know the gospel when I was a teenager through English missionaries who had started a work among the children and youth. Several lively preachers passed through the traditional churches giving birth to a revival among the young people. We loved to gather together on Saturday evenings to sing and pray.

Crammed into a small parish hall that night, we waited impatiently for the meeting to begin. It would be led by a team from Youth With A Mission that had come specially from Lausanne to invite young

Christians to participate in an evangelistic camp in Paris that summer, 1973. Daniel Schaerer, first-generation YWAMer and leader of our youth group, had organized this event, since he had participated in the 1972 Summer of Service during the Munich Olympic Games.

It was that evening in Forbach that I saw Linda for the first time. I still remember her, guitar in hand, with her beautiful red hair flowing over her shoulders. Something peaceful came from her, a calm strength, drawn from a deeper source. The team followed her unobtrusive lead. The atmosphere was charged with a contagious love for God.

The evening was a success, and many youth decided to participate in the Summer of Service. Since I had committed to be a counselor in another Christian camp which would take place at the same time, I was disappointed that I could not join them this time around.

Two years after that memorable evening, however, I was off to Lausanne to join YWAM for three months . . . which has turned into thirty years!

At one point when a music team was being assembled for a tour, Linda came to see me. She simply asked me to pray and seek God's will regarding this project. So I did. I then found myself on board for the musical and choreographed presentation, *Si mon peuple* (*If My People*). This performance was based on the prophetic message taken from the well-known biblical passage, 2 Chronicles 7:14, "If my people will humble themselves . . ."

In the beginning, my role was to be mostly pastoral and organizational, but this also became my opportunity to write my first music compositions. When I sang them to the planning team, I received a lot of encouragement and counsel.

I also had some internal battles as I was confronted with my own limits, not having had very much formal music training. We had been listening to an excellent recording of English songs and it seemed to me that they were light-years in advance and that my work was mediocre in comparison. I'll always remember this remark from Linda, "You know, you don't need to do the same thing they are doing. Just do something that is you!" It was the word I needed to hear and it liberated me.

I am thankful to Linda for discerning my potential and permitting me to get my foot in the stirrup. Discovering new talent in people and encouraging them are among her most precious gifts. And she does it so naturally. As I travel through the French-speaking world today, I regularly meet Christians who have been touched by a word or a meeting with Linda.

In Switzerland

Linda has played an important role in kicking off the worship movement in French-speaking Switzerland. In the preceding chapters we read how the songbook *J'aime l'Eternel* (*I Love the Lord*) was born. Its impact still continues today in the churches. Even groups that initially showed a certain hostility to anything that was new came to adopt various aspects of the worship styles created during those years.

I remember our evening meetings in the Hotel School's auditorium at Chalet-à-Gobet—Linda seated at their magnificent grand piano, me behind my guitar, Tom Bloomer with his waxed moustache, Cynthia at his side to translate, leading one of these revolutionary times of worship. This internationally known Hotel School of Lausanne rented us their auditorium when we could no longer accommodate the number of visitors at our YWAM center. People were so thirsty for worship that they came from all over the region in all types of weather to attend these meetings between heaven and earth.

Once a person has tasted the marvelous presence of God, he is never content to experience it only every other week. And there was no reason for us YWAMers to keep such a precious treasure to ourselves. Consequently, many churches went on to develop this type of worship in their own services.

When the TEMA missionary conferences[1] started in Lausanne, worship was given a central place and Linda was asked to be the coordinator. Since it was a European-wide gathering for thousands of people, it was no small affair to handle. It necessitated choosing songs in multiple languages and setting up worship groups capable of leading an international audience. The thorny questions of style and differences in traditions, according to the countries and denominations, also had to be considered. On top of that, Linda prepared a songbook with vocal

1. See chapter 10.

arrangements and a recording, because the organizers desired that the participants return home with the worship from the Congress. Let it be said, this very taxing job was a non-paid position, often requiring Linda to work late into the night.

How many youth responded to the invitations of various speakers saying, "Here am I, Lord, send me!"? No one knows exactly, but we saw them stand up by the hundreds. There is no doubt that the worship times stirred a favorable heart attitude to hear and obey the voice of the Master of the harvest.

Today Linda and her husband Tom continue to travel to French-speaking churches and youth groups, sharing their love for Jesus. They passionately invest themselves in Alpha Courses, following the marching orders of Youth With A Mission from Matthew 28:18, to make disciples of all nations. This program, which proposes faith in God to the unchurched world, has seen good results in Switzerland. It is wonderful to see Tom and Linda's faces light up when they talk about a neighbor coming to faith in Christ, or to hear their concerned tone of voice when a young Christian is going through difficult times.

In the World

The French-speaking world is vast. In Africa alone nearly thirty countries speak French as their official language. It serves as the link between nations internationally, as well as internally, since dozens of languages are spoken inside each country.

Linda has never traveled to French-speaking Africa, but her influence in an indirect way has been enormous. It was in 1998, during a worship seminar in Gabon where I had been invited to speak, that I took stock of this phenomena. Several years earlier, a group of Christian high schoolers had started meeting together. Listening to the first cassettes produced by YWAM Lausanne, they were blown away by this dimension of worship that they had not previously encountered.

The YWAM teams who had produced these cassettes under Linda's direction didn't have the impression that they were accomplishing something extraordinary, but on the other side of the world they were initiating a revolution in the hearts of many. Their impact on these teenage students produced a revival among the youth and the founding of several dozen churches. I had the joy of leading a time of worship in one of their assemblies with three thousand people present! Of course YWAM was not the only one to influence worship, but at that point in time you could count the number of French worship ministries on the fingers of one hand.

Ten years after that trip, my wife, Maryse, and I were again in Africa. We had been invited to the home of missionary friends, Remy and Cathy Moret, for a special evening with an army colonel and his wife. During supper the colonel told us about his first steps toward the Lord during a performance of *L'Ami* (*The Friend*), an evangelistic street drama.

This presentation had been created for one of the Summer of Service outreaches in Avignon, France. The soundtrack, recorded in Lausanne, contained songs and musical interludes describing the broken heart of God and the plan of salvation. We find several of Linda's compositions therein and of course her touch in the musical arrangements. Many teams have used it as a tool for evangelism, notably in Africa, where it was extremely popular.

After dessert, in a moment of great nostalgia, we continued our evening with the colonel, his wife and our missionary friends by singing as many of the songs that we could remember from *L'Ami*, accompanied by my guitar.

How many hearts were opened to the love of the Father while viewing one of these performances? Only heaven knows, but until then, we have the joy from time to time to see some of the fruit during our earthly journey.

Personal

A fruitful life never happens without battles. This may be obvious for certain people, but honestly, there is a price to pay for following the Lord. There is no flourishing ministry without sacrifices.

I have known Linda during times of success and mountain top experiences, but I have also walked beside her in seasons of frailty, notably when the doctors announced to her that she had a chronic illness of which the outcome was uncertain. It was during this time that I saw her continue to worship and rely on the Lord who had called her, despite her weakness.

Crossing a desert reveals hidden motivations and allows light to shine on old wounds that have never been treated. I observed more than several times when Linda made the choice to confront rather than run, to approach the Father of Light rather than make excuses. The secret of great men and women of God is not that they are perfect, but that they face their trials, illness and sin with one goal . . . to bring glory to God. Each time that Linda's road was rough, she came through it with greater maturity and authority.

What does her story teach us?

If you enjoy reading biographies like I do, you have certainly been stimulated and edified by stories of exceptional men and women. I must admit that I admire the abilities and commitment of so many of them, considering them worthy of praise, but realize how far I am trailing behind them.

What I find wonderful about Linda's adventure of faith is that it is within anyone's grasp. Rather than holding on to my securities, if I dare to take those little steps of obedience and trust in God, just like she did, I too can have a marvelous destiny with God.

Who could have foreseen that a young girl from a normal family, lost in the cornfields of mid-west America, would have such a huge influence on the French-speaking world?

When we respond to the call of God, miracles happen and things that are impossible for men become possible with God. The few loaves and fishes from my small basket become food that the Lord multiplies to satisfy the hungry.

May this testimony convince each reader that there is no greater joy than saying yes to the marvelous plan of God. Our destiny is not limited to our social condition, to our talents, or to our IQ. In spite of economic crises or fears expressed by our family members, this is the best thing I could wish for you.

Rolf Schneider
Director of French Music Department
Youth With A Mission

Timeline: Forty Years of YWAM Switzerland

1969   First School of Evangelism (SOE) at Château d'Oex, Switzerland. At the end of the year YWAM moves into the former Hôtel du Golf, at Chalet-à-Gobet, which becomes the first center and the second SOE begins. Within a few years, this ministry pioneered YWAM centers in more than twenty countries of Europe and Africa.

First Swiss and European YWAMer, Rudi Lack

1971   Beginning of French Ministries with Joe and Judi Portale

1972   One thousand YWAMers participate in the Summer of Service (SOS) at the Munich Olympics

1973   SOS in Paris with 330 young people

YWAM French Publications is born with the printing of its first two books

First SOE in French at Chalet-à-Gobet

1974   First edition of the French songbook *J'aime l'Eternel* (*I Love the Lord*) by Linda Panci-McGowen

Sunday evening worship meetings are opened to the public at Chalet-à-Gobet

Regular fellowship with the Billy Graham team, who prepared and led the Lausanne Congress on World Evangelism

1975   YWAM participates at Eurofest in Brussels, a youth festival gathering five thousand people from across Europe

First Discipleship Training School (DTS) in English at Chalet-à-Gobet, led by Albert Joly

First evangelistic outreach in Africa, with Joe Portale's team crossing the Sahara

In the following years, evangelism teams from Switzerland were sent to Africa, Canada, Spain, Argentina, Madagascar, the Reunion Islands, ex-USSR, Eastern Europe, India, Himalayas, France, Italy, Belgium, etc.

Mobile worship teams criss-cross French-speaking Europe as well as discipleship training teams with video teaching cassettes

1976   Launch of the first YWAM base in French-speaking Africa at M'Pouto, Ivory Coast, led by Joe Portale

Tom and Cynthia Bloomer become the directors of YWAM French Ministries

Departure of 180 young missionaries from French-speaking Europe to testify during the Montreal Olympic Games

First recording of songs from the songbook *J'aime l'Eternel*

Begin worship evenings at the Hotel School, eventually followed by regular worship celebrations at the Palais de Beaulieu in Lausanne, as well as in Neuchâtel, Yverdon, Reconvilier, Bulle, Martigny, and "Worship Concerts" in Yverdon for the Suisse Romande (French-speaking Switzerland)

Eliane Lack and Denis Ducatel project Billy Graham films in the Suisse Romande. The film *Joni* draws ten thousand people to local theaters

1977   First French-speaking DTS at Chalet-à-Gobet, led by Daniel Schaerer

Creation of the musical *Si mon peuple* (*If My People*), performances given throughout French-speaking Europe

SOS in Vevey during the Fête des Vignerons (Wine Maker's Festival) with 444 young people

1978   Ship ministry launched from Chalet-à-Gobet with the

purchase of the *Anastasis*. It becomes Mercy Ships, led by Don and Deyon Stephens

Forty young people sent out from Chalet-à-Gobet to pioneer YWAM France in Charmes and later at Gault-la-Forêt, with Daniel Schaerer as director

1979   First counseling seminar at Chalet-à-Gobet with Heinz and Elsie Schoenhoff and Charlotte Fuchs (now Bruderer)

SOS in Avignon, France, organized from Chalet-à-Gobet, 260 participants

1980   Acquisition of "La Maison" in Burtigny under the leadership of Heinz and Jolinette Suter

Numerous Swiss join European YWAMers for the Olympic games outreach in the ex-USSR and for ministry in other Soviet block countries

Production of the musical *L'Ami* (*the Friend*), played first in Avignon then in many French-speaking countries

1981   SOS in Geneva, Switzerland

1982   First SOS in French-speaking Africa for five weeks in Ouaga-dougou with 110 Europeans and 110 Africans; conversion of Noufou who later becomes the leader of YWAM Burkina Faso

1983   Creation of the musical *Le Chanteur* (*the Singer*), performed at the SOS in Avignon, France

First French/Italian DTS at Burtigny with Enos and Marguer-ita Nolli and family

1984   Birth of "Fabricants de joie" (Joy-makers) with Louise Neuen-schwander (now Aubry)

And a tour with the musical *Machine à Musique* (*Music Machine*)

Raymond and Irène Serex are sent from Chalet-à-Gobet to open a YWAM center in Burkina Faso

Launch of YWAM Mali in Sikasso by Jean-Patrick and Ruth Perrin

Bruce and Barbara Thompson begin counseling schools

and seminars (which will widely influence French-speaking Europe)

1985   Birth of music group VISA with Rolf Schneider and Philippe Bogdan performing evangelistic concerts in the French-speaking world. The group continued to evolve and minister until 2013.

Pioneering of YWAM Togo at Agou by Raymond and Irène Serex, with the launching of the first DTS in West Africa led by Jean-Patrick and Ruth Perrin

"Walk of the Cross" teams from the four corners of Switzerland do an evangelistic walk, finishing with a large gathering at the Federal Palace in Bern where Arthur Blessit speaks

YWAM is established in the Tessin (Italian-speaking part of Switzerland) and then Italy in 1987 by Enos Nolli

1986   First SOS of "Fabricants de joie" in France organized by Louise with Jean-Claude and Isabelle Serex

Opening of YWAM Cameroon by Salu and Annelyse Daka sent from Chalet-à-Gobet

1987   Heinz Suter appointed YWAM Suisse Romande director

"Hospital Christian Fellowship" gives their Einigen center to YWAM, with Rudi and Eliane Lack as leaders

First Easter camp by "Fabricants de joie"

1988   YWAM acquires the properties of Châtel and Bugnaux-sur-Rolle, establishing a center for counseling schools

Creation of Medair by Josiane and Erik Volkmar in collaboration with YWAM Mercy Ministries, Medications for Africa, and Mission Aviation Fellowship; furnishing emergency aid to remote and devastated communities

1989   Worldwide "Torch Run," evangelism teams carry a flame across every nation

The Swiss Council of YWAM is formed, bringing together the French and German- speaking Swiss leaders

Birth of "Fabricants de joie" in Africa by Geneviève De Pury

Daniel Schaerer appointed coordinator of YWAM French-speaking ministries worldwide

Sylvain Freymond develops live praise recordings and leads praise teams throughout the French-speaking world

1990   Elaine Lack becomes coordinator of YWAM Switzerland; presiding the Swiss Council

Maiden voyage of the ship "*Anastasis*" to Togo, West Africa

1991   "Porteurs de vie" (Messengers of Life), teams of evangelists, launched by Carlo and Michèle Brugnoli

David Durham with François and Christine Reymond produce the first *Face à face* (Face to Face) album, which initiates a new series of recordings by YWAM French Publications

First School of Worship in French, pioneered by Sylvain Freymond at Chalet-à-Gobet

1992   French Music Ministry moves to Yverdon and changes name to "Département musique"

1993   Closure of YWAM Chalet-à-Gobet due to renovations

1994   Loren and Darlene Cunningham return to Chalet-à-Gobet to rebuild the center

GENESIS, teaching by video conferencing, begins from Chalet-à-Gobet with a link to Budapest. By 2009, connected to more than eighty YWAM locations in the world.

Creation of Mercy Ministries Association by Scott Morey, Erik Spruyt, and Marc Stettler, serving the poor and supporting development projects

1997   The Alpha Course begins in French-speaking Switzerland, led by Olivier Fleury

1998   Launching of Principles in Child and Youth Ministry school at Burtigny, led by Guy and Joële Zeller

Niko camps (character and team building) and Tilt (preparation for adolescence) started by Fabricants de joie ministry

1999   Quartier Libre (neighborhood evangelism and activities for children), initiated by Didier and Eve Crelier, spreads through the Suisse Romande

First camp of radio controlled model planes for fathers and sons, led by Carlo Brugnoli

2001   First seminar with Earl Pitts in collaboration with the Men's Forum, teaching biblical principles for finance and business management

2002   "Family Resource Ministries" pioneered by Paul and Geneviève Marsh

InTouch camps begin in Suisse Romande with Roy and Shirley Jones

Creation of Antizone, street activities for teenagers, led by Marjorie Wäfler

2004   Daniel Schaerer passes on the role of overseeing YWAM French Ministries to Raymond Serex

Opening of House of Worship in Pomy by Sylvain Freymond to promote 24/7 worship

2008   Appointing of Olivier Fleury as the leader of YWAM Suisse Romande

2009   Forty-year celebration of YWAM in Switzerland

YWAM French Publications continues to supply CDs and books to the French-speaking world; seventy-seven CDs produced, forty-four book titles, music scores, DVDs, four song books of which hundreds of thousands of copies of *J'aime l'Eternel* sold

*Summer of
Service music
team, 1975*

*Philippe, Sue
and Linda*

Multi-media team recruits for Olympic Outreach, 1976

Marlyse, Max, Roselyne, and Carlo stuff envelopes

Micheline Le Briquer

YWAM center in Dunham, Canada

Girls' dormitory at Montreal Outreach, 1976

Linda and Gloria eating fondue

*Celebrating
Tom Bloomer's
birthday, with
Cynthia*

*Rudi and
Eliane Lack
at YWAM
Einigen*

L'équipe *Si mon Peuple 1977 - 1978*

PHOTOS : MICHELINE LE BRIQUER

Micheline Le Briquer

YWAM center at Le Gault, France, 1978

Micheline Le Briquer

Daniel and Maguy Schaerer, first French national leaders

Dominique Pelou

*YWAMers
praying beside
the Rhone*

Micheline Le Briquer

*The Bridge of
Avignon*

Micheline Le Briquer

Rolf leads worship at the Palace of the Popes, 1979

Micheline Le Briquer

Daniel and Gabriel perform L'Ami *in Geneva, 1981*

Dominique Pelou

Cynthia in L'Ami

Micheline Le Briquer

Linda taking a mini-nap

Rolf and Maryse Schneider with Linda

Music Team at Ouchy, Lausanne, 1981

Dominique Pelou

YWAM center at Burtigny

Dominique Pelou

*Music Team
at Ouchy,
Lausanne*

Dominique Pelou

*Jocelyne,
working in
French Music
office*

*Music camp
with Joseph
Broussaudier*

*Singing at
the arena in
Nimes, 1981*

Paul Schilliger

Linda &
Tom Panci,
December 31,
1985

Linda with
Cynthia and
Jocelyne

Linda with
Tom and
brothers, John
and Joe

*Celebrating
40 years of
marriage for
Mom & Dad,
1986*

*Schneider
family*

Micheline Le Briquer

*Dedication of
Linda's CD,
2003*

My 60th birthday party in Swiss Alps

YWAM French Publications committee, 2012

Dad & Mom, my greatest supporters

Guy Barblan,
director of
Psalmodia